MOTI
THR
INCENTIVES

A Daily Telegraph
BUSINESS ENTERPRISE BOOK

MOTIVATING THROUGH INCENTIVES

Published by Telegraph Publications,
Peterborough Court, At South Quay,
181 Marsh Wall, London E14 9SR

Series Editor: Marlene Garsia

Typeset by MHL Typesetting Ltd., Coventry.
Printed by R.J. Acford, Chichester.

British Library Cataloguing in Publication Data
Gazzard, Ken
Motivating for profit: making the most of incentive marketing.
1. Sales personnel—Salaries, commissions, etc. 2. Incentives in industry
I. Title II. Gray-Forton, Geoffrey
658.3′225 HF5439.7

ISBN 0-86367-079-2

Acknowledgements

There were a number of people who kindly helped us in the preparation of this text. In particular we would like to thank Barbara Cox, David Hughes, Brian Morgan and John Mulford for their valued assistance.

Contents

Introduction

As almost any hypnotist will tell you – especially one whose skills are devoted to therapeutic use – you cannot, even by hypnosis, make people do what they do not want to do. In that respect, hypnosis and the management of people at work are similar – at least in a free-enterprise democracy. The art and science of motivation, as described in this book, is therefore not to make people at work do what management wants, but to make them want to do the job role given; to give them an incentive which makes them want to accomplish their task.

Now this is where, if one is not very careful, the major misunderstanding regarding incentives and motivation can arise – and it is a misunderstanding which, if not eliminated at an early stage, remains firmly fixed in the memory permanently clouding the issue. In order to illustrate this danger, it is necessary only to scan the advertisements in the marketing press for 'incentives'. The overwhelming majority will be for items such as instant cameras, fine china collections, boats and trailers, golf clubs, hi-fi and videos – you name it and it is there. Yet incentives are not solely material or objects. The definition most commonly found in dictionaries refers to an incentive as 'that which incites to action'.

Motivation through incentives is also international. Marketing legislation may vary from country to country but, within the world of marketing and motivation, the traits displayed by people wherever you go in the world are the same deep down. And motivated people are more profitable people, both for you, for themselves, and for your business. But what is an incentive? How do you decide what to use and for whom? Let us start with the first question.

An incentive is a decision-provoking thought, a concept in the mind which leads to an action. It has always been the same. Incentives are an induced condition of the mind. And the influence of thoughts and mental images are the technology of motivation.

What this book has to include is human psychology, behavioural science and, here and there, a touch of sociology. But upon this foundation it builds an infinite variety of motivational structures, varying from the simple to the highly complex, from minimal costs (can a £500 incentive budget be anything else?) up to seven figure sums which need to be spent on highly complex award-giving programmes. The term 'infinite' variety is used deliberately; you take over from what is actually written and the end result is as much your creation as it is the book's inspiration.

The case studies in this book include a few abject failures as well as several fêted triumphs. These are not there to be copied but to be learnt from. They illustrate merely a few of the practical applications of simple principles which other people, just like you and facing problems just as daunting, either have discovered or have had revealed to them. Some techniques which could conceivably be described as 'motivating through incentives' have resolutely been excluded: consumer incentives, for instance.

Now there was a temptation that was hard to resist! The average consumer promotion, however ingenious or flamboyant, does not make the average consumer do anything extra. What the Bingo game, the scratch-off card and the fore-court coupon achieve is not a true incentive; they are merely inducements. They motivate, true, but to direct consumer action (already motivated) to one brand rather than another. The motorist needing petrol cannot physically buy more than he uses, the housewife cannot make her family eat more breakfast – the decision which has been motivated is not as to whether one should act or not, it is which way one should act, having already decided on the action.

Many other concepts, if not excluded, are given far less prominence than they might appear to deserve. Team building, leadership, conferences are given very little space indeed. Business gifts, too, receive only a mention, since they are in truth 'sales promotion' rather than the act of motivating people at work to improve their performance.

1 The history and meaning of incentive marketing

Motivating others to do what you want them to do goes back thousands of years. The sponsors may have been Phoenician overlords and the objective the improvement of agricultural output. The concept of incentives as a means of motivation is as old as civilisation itself. The methods of achieving the objectives have many different applications and they have changed and become more sophisticated over the years. However, the objective – to create and achieve a goal which would not be attained without the provision and influence of an incentive award – remains with us today. On the evidence available it would appear that there are now more opportunities to participate in some form of incentive activity than at any time, and the rewards are more acceptable to society as a whole.

At this stage it will be beneficial to differentiate between two types of basic incentive. The first is termed commercial motivation, for example the use of incentive programmes within commercial organisations, and the second is consumer motivation, for example the system introduced by the original Co-operative Wholesale Society (CWS).

At the turn of the century, the CWS introduced a system which was based on a savings scheme. They gave tin coins to shoppers which represented a percentage of their purchases. The coins could be exchanged only at CWS stores, which led inevitably to customer (and brand) loyalty. Even though there were many instances where some goods were priced higher than their competitors, the incentive to cash in the coin tokens undoubtedly drew new customers and retained others who might have been tempted to shop elsewhere. The idea was soon copied by many other outlets including multiple stores and small corner shops. Thus the trading stamp was conceived, although few people realised it. However, we are now drifting into an area of 'sales promotion', and the temptation to expand further must again be resisted. Nevertheless, the text will examine the influence of trading stamps on 'motivating through incentives' when various award media used in incentive campaigns are discussed.

Into the 20TH Century

It is almost certain that the realisation of the need for organised, professional incentive activity as we now know it, originated in 1922. It began with Elton F MacDonald. At this time he was working as an assistant in a luggage store in Dayton, Ohio. One day the sales manager of a local manufacturing organisation called into the store and indicated that he wished to buy a number of briefcases which he would offer as prizes to his sales representatives in his company's forthcoming sales contest. After concluding the sale, MacDonald – then only 18 years old – suggested it might be a good idea to offer luggage or other leather goods as prizes in a follow-up contest so as to generate further momentum. This sale was also made. Thereafter followed the production and distribution of a leaflet which incorporated a number of prize items, varying in

value, which the contest winners could choose, depending on the level of their achievements. So emerged the first professional incentive company in modern history.

The successes achieved by MacDonald-sourced merchandise in the form of different incentive programmes soon became widespread throughout the US. Only a few years elapsed before the mighty automotive manufacturers in Detroit called him in to structure programmes for their dealer networks throughout the country. As time went by, MacDonald's clients, particularly the multi-national companies, exported the incentive concept to their overseas operations, so EFM, the company that had grown up around Elton MacDonald, spread its business across the Atlantic. They established their operations in the UK and in Europe during the late 1950s. Realising the potential opened up by EFM, Sperry & Hutchinson of New York soon established their subsidiary company, Incentive Awards in the UK. At the same time the British-owned Green Shield Trading Stamp Company started motivational programme activities with the formation of Performance Awards Limited. Further infiltration from the US occurred in the early 1970s when Maritz Incorporated of St Louis extended their services into Europe. Incentive companies were now firmly established, not only in the US but throughout Europe.

The *modus operandi* these organisations either brought with them or adopted comprised glossy, up-market catalogues featuring desirable merchandise of wide-ranging value. The items offered were priced, not in monetary value, but in a special currency designed, printed and issued by the incentive company. These were called Prize Points, Award Credits, Award Points, etc. There were already a number of mail-order catalogues available, but they were considered less suitable for motivational purposes in terms of their quality of content and their presentation.

Top quality brand names were featured prominently in the incentive companies' catalogues, on the premise that neither the campaign sponsors nor their participants would wish to be identified with anything less than the best. The catalogues featured semi-luxury items which the participants would feel they would not normally purchase or be able to afford. Obviously, a great deal of expertise went into catalogue design and format – and into the selection of featured items. The range was wide and included sports goods, cameras, household appliances, furniture, garden equipment, fashion items, kitchen utensils and quality toys, all ideally suited for a consumer-oriented society.

Wherever possible, a copy of the catalogue or Award Collection was despatched to each incentive programme participant's home, since the necessity was seen by the incentive companies to motivate not only the employees but also their families. This factor greatly influenced the items included in the catalogues. It also proved that analysis undertaken by the specialists was correct. The tasteful nature of the promotional materials tended to invoke co-operation among the family to help achieve the desired items.

First in the US and later in Europe, it became more apparent to the incentive company professionals that merchandise, although by far the most cost-effective award medium so far introduced, needed some other ingredient. A new award was called for which, while allowing the majority to benefit from catalogue items, placed the real high fliers in a class of their own – a recognised elite – and gave them something which they would never forget. And so incentive travel was born.

It was in the mid-1950s; the war had been over for several years, and the European continent was becoming an attractive venue. Tourism was new and expanding and the age of the jet-setter was dawning.

Given the proper proportion of a sizeable overall incentive budget, the top few in the performance league table could – together with their wives who had helped and co-operated in their success – enjoy each other's company and that of a senior host couple from the company's management on a VIP holiday of their dreams.

Having seen the powerful impact of group incentive travel on campaign participants, the experts found that by offering the facility of using the existing award 'currency' as either full or part-payment for inclusive tours or package holidays, they brought overseas holidays within the reach of a far greater proportion of the work force. The quality of these family holiday awards were no match, of course, for the grandeur and luxury enjoyed by the top few during their group celebration in, for example, Hawaii, Bangkok or the West Indies.

However, from a dream holiday of a lifetime to part-paid eight days on the Costa Brava, incentive travel was here to stay. And the ingenuity which goes into its organisation will be demonstrated in a later chapter.

You may have gained the impression that all the developments and refinements referred to in this potted history of incentives was directed towards sales people, to motivate them to achieve results over and above targets or quotas. Initially there was a strong tendency to restrict incentive programmes almost solely to sales personnel. From the early years right up to the 1970s the incentive companies and their clients alike became accustomed to sales incentive programmes. Today, however, all categories and levels of management and employees are given opportunities in which to participate. The factory or shop floor is now just as likely to be included in an incentive programme as are the senior management of a company. This is partially due to the fact that nowadays a greater range of measurable objectives can be considered for inclusion when forming an overall corporate programme.

The most far-reaching impact on the growth of the incentive industry was brought about by expanding outside the confines of the sponsoring client's own employed personnel.

For example, whereas generally 25 per cent of the overall budgets for incentive programmes were directed at the company employee, anything up to 75 per cent was actually utilised to fund programmes for the once-removed participants, wholesalers, distributors, dealers and retailers. The automotive industry is a perfect example. A motor company employing 20 or 30 salesmen of its own will have 500 or more dealerships, each an independent company employing possibly a dozen or more employees, not to mention the dealer's managing director, chairman or proprietor, and other auxiliary members of staff.

Finally, one 'quirk' of this already curious science is the MI5 approach, a kind of secrecy which surrounds much of the industry's activities and results, particularly in the area of sales and marketing incentive programmes. For example, the safety director of a leading petroleum company was delighted to lecture in public on the structure, success and cost-effectiveness of the company's 'Safety is No Accident' campaign – even at meetings with rival oil companies' safety personnel. But sales and marketing is a far more cloak-and-dagger affair.

Motivation in the twentieth century has grown from one man's idea into a world-wide industry and profession. It could not possibly have achieved such stature unless it were built upon a sure and firm foundation. And yet it had been flourishing for around 40 years before its practitioners had any inkling of what that foundation was. It was, when it came, an eye-opening revelation.

2 The psychological and behavioural disciplines behind motivation

Psychology and behavioural scientists find it difficult to inspire the general public into any enthusiasm for the results of their theoretical findings concerning motivation.

'How can you possibly ignore this?' 'This is the very stuff of which you are made – this is what makes you tick!' These statements are often heard complaining about the general lack of interest. But why such a lack of interest? Perhaps it is the style or lack of it, the terminology, the plethora of references to other works and the sheer length of the volumes that are produced that combine to motivate yawns, instead of yearnings to know more.

However, the *raison d'être* of motivating people at work for profit is what causes them to tick a little faster, more consistently, and more productively. Discovering what makes people tick is the first essential step towards accelerating this rate. Therefore there will be no copious quotations from learned tomes, no long drawn-out records of experiments with rats, hamsters or Pavlov's dogs and no jargon; merely an outline of the essential facts and discoveries in the field of human needs and desires which the motivator must use, to his own and his company's benefit, in improving the performance of the people for whom he is responsible.

Towards the end of the 1960s several of the major incentive companies, realising that the technology had to have some form of discipline, began to study the psychology of motivation. They discovered what they had been doing for a generation was correct simply because it worked Unknowingly, perhaps, what they had been doing was science-based. It was this new-found knowledge which subsequently inspired them to develop programmes around the deep-seated needs of the participants. However, a degree in psychology is not needed in order to be aware that, in the average workforce, there are three groups of achievers, and three levels of performance.

There are the high flyers, the average performers, and the passengers. The first and most prized are the high flyers, the super-sales people, the production target-beaters, the workaholics who can be relied on to do an excellent job. These are the people for whom you advertise in the quality media. Their performance is generally above the level of the ambient norm of humanity that surround them. The one regret is that, although you really need a full complement of such producers, they normally comprise only 10 to 15 per cent of the people you actually employ.

Between 70 per cent and 80 per cent of your staff exert themselves sufficiently on your behalf to equal the ambient norm. What that norm is at any one time will decide whether you consider them the backbone of your company or the average performers.

Inevitably, there are those whose output represents less than the surrounding norm. Whether these are passengers or potential high flyers depends on their input more than their output; with the right training (and motivation?) some could well ascend through the levels and shine; others – it has to be said – might be in the wrong company or even in the wrong occupation, perhaps. Sociology has a remarkable apt term for them, 'Those in transit'.

Probably everyone in supervision or management realises this. What the psychologist and the behavioural scientist does is to give reasons why each kind of person performs at that level, why they exist in the proportions indicated and why different motives are at work at different consciousness levels within their make-up.

Schools of thought

Maslow's pyramid

There are many different schools of thought on the levels of motivation. The best known one is the Maslow pyramid. [See page 12, Figure 1: Maslow's Pyramid of Needs.]

The Maslow theory contends that once a person has satisfied the lowest level of need, the one above it becomes the dominant need, and so on. The apex of the triangle represents the ultimate goal which is as much spiritual as material.

The highest aspirations of which human nature is capable are not excluded, so Maslow's pyramid is highly commendable, but in reality his premise of progression towards an ideal falls down – frequently! Notably in the current climate of uncertainty, one's needs can move up and down between base and apex almost weekly, while in the minor influences of life, including life at work, a daily roller-coaster ride through the range is by no means unheard of. With or without Maslow, however, the pattern is now established.

What is clear is that man is indeed motivated on three levels: the Conscious, the Pre-conscious and the Unconscious. Conscious motivation, by its very nature, is obvious to all, including the person who is motivated (or de-motivated!).

Figure 1: Maslow's 'Pyramid of Needs'

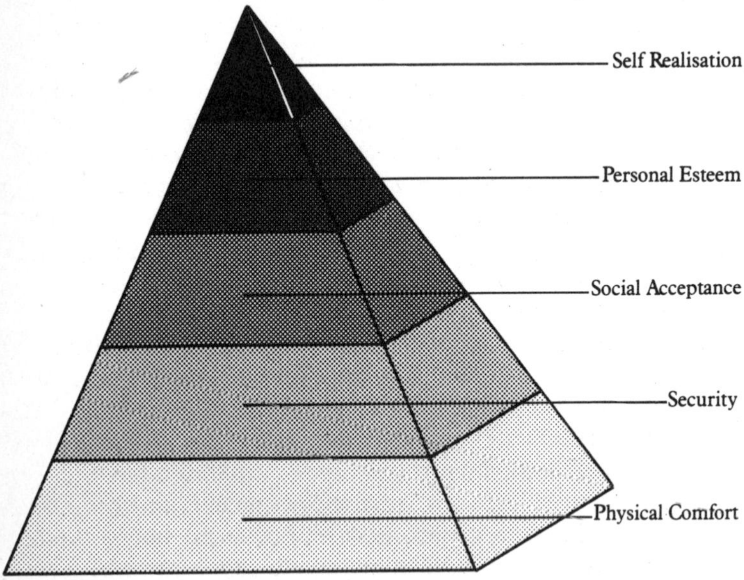

∴ SELF REALISATION
= Does one's own thing.

PERSONAL ESTEEM
= Recognition by a group.

SOCIAL ACCEPTANCE
= In a group or society.

SECURITY
= Maintenance of physical comfort.

PHYSICAL COMFORT
= Basic food and shelter.

Incidentally, there is surely no such thing as de-motivation? The opposite of motivation (the existence of a motive) must be understood to be the absence of a motive, which is not understood by the term de-motivation. So what should the terminology be?

Herzberg motivation and hygiene factors
In the US this question was addressed by Professor Fredrick Herzberg, who proposed the existence of two kinds of stimuli; positive and negative. As his work was closely allied to his occupation of Public Health Inspector he called the positive influences Motivation Factors and the negative stimuli Hygiene Factors. His research, carried out among several thousand people at work, revealed one or two surprises.

A composite of the factors that are involved in causing job satisfaction and job dissatisfaction was drawn from samples of 1,685 employees. The results indicated that motivations were the primary cause of satisfaction, and hygiene factors the primary cause of unhappiness at work. The employees, studied in 12 different investigations, covered a wide spectrum from lower level supervisors to teachers and accountants. The interviewees were asked what job events had occurred in their work that had led to extreme satisfaction or extreme dissatisfaction on their part.

Among the motivation factors were achievement, recognition, responsibility, personal growth, interesting work and so on, while prominent among the hygiene factors (the negative motivators) were company policy, pay, working conditions and the way in which the company was administered. One fact, however, cannot be too highly stressed. Removal of the negative hygiene factor produces positive motivation while on the other hand, blandly acceding to pay and hours demands or changing company policy and procedures will achieve no permanent improvement in performance whatsoever.

Herzberg's findings still hold good today, but they are not nearly enough. Conscious motivation is merely on the surface, instantly recognisable because of that but useless on its own; thus research must probe more deeply. Pre-conscious influences are, understandably, slightly more subtle but still recognisable provided we, or someone whom we trust, can see them for what they are. Our reactions to pre-conscious motivations are decided, in their varying proportions, by the time we are six years old. These pre-conscious motivations are three in number, each classed as a need or hunger. In turn, this need urges an action and a reason for acting and blended together forms a personality. The three hungers are sensation, recognition and structure.

Sensation hunger is typified by the need to experience, physically and emotionally, feelings that stimulate: for example, empty space beneath the hang-glider, the roar of a powerful engine and the lonely silence of the mountain top. Virtually every fairground ride caters for sensation hunger.

Recognition hunger is the need of the gregarious, few of whom would perhaps recognise it themselves, while even fewer will admit to it. As we shall see, the satisfaction of recognition hunger is a major motivational achievement.

A more subtle feeling is produced by structure hunger. Those in whom it is dominant tend not to be found in sales forces but in the decision-making process. Such people are happier behind a chess board than a Formula One steering wheel.

The most important fact to remember about the pre-conscious hungers – and remember it you must if you wish to motivate profitably – is that all three are present in every human being, in infinitely varying proportions. Frequently one of them dominates. But if you can spot their make-up in each of your employees you then have taken a great leap forward towards motivation.

Not only have you vastly increased your incentive skills but you have learned a vital lesson, which is 'people do things for their own reasons, not yours!'.

And still there is the innermost level; unconscious motivation. You can recognise your own positive/negative conscious motives, others can perceive your pre-conscious hungers for you, but it takes a trained specialist to identify your unconscious needs.

Unconscious needs

There are three unconscious needs, and their names are associated with the first few years of life. Expressed starkly in the clinical terminology of Freud, Jung and Adler, they sound most awkward and uncomfortable to a red-blooded adult:

- To have a mother;
- To act so as to please mother and father;
- To be like father (this applies to girls as well as boys – frequently more so!).

Before relating these terms to a bearded welder, or a macho sales representative or an aggressive red-head in the regional office, you must discover how these infant needs crossed the divide into adulthood.

'Mother' is represented by the peer group. This can be the team, the department, the shift – even the company. It relates to any association that cares for and surrounds you. Although the need for a 'mother' is strong, you are now an independent being and as such you have the ability to go out and choose a 'mother' if you feel (or are persuaded) that your present one is failing in any way. Still further, if your union 'step-mother' is failing you, you can actually create your own!

The company is needed for survival, comfort and the satisfaction of psychological requirements. And just as you were part of your mother, needing her as an external provider, you now need to be part of a group. As an individual member, you please the group with which you most identify.

In the definition of the unconscious needs, father becomes the one to whom 'mother' looks to for leadership, protection and the family authority. In other words the foremen, the charge-hand, the manager, director, even the chairman. You need to be like the one who is your group's leader; to emulate the one who emerges as your 'father image', with his sense o direction, his independence, ability to protect, and the mastery he has over his own destiny.

Perhaps the best illustration of the relationshi between conscious, pre-conscious and unconscious motivations is that of a young boy who, because he is loved by his parents and acts to please them both, is given his first bicycle for hi birthday. The boy seeks the leadership of his father for the first, wobbly lesson and, at the right stage of progress, father lets him 'go it alone'. Off he pedals and inside five minutes he tearfully limps back, with a buckled wheel and a grazed knee. To his father's question he complains 'I fell off my bike!' Father, instead of anger displays quiet reassurance, points out that he, too, has suffered set-backs under similar circumstances when young pride, briefly satisfiec by new sensations and a desire for recognition, has taken a tumble.

The father, and perhaps the boy, may have realised and accepted this pre-conscious assessment, but what neither of them have perceived i that the boy, in setting off on his own, was trying to emulate his father. Suddenly he was independent, mobile, in control of direction and speed and, to some extent, master of his own destiny. However, his dream was shattered just as it was assuming reality and there, deep inside his innermost, unconscious self, lay the fundamental source of his tears. You know, of course, your role in this imaginary tale.

You should also appreciate that in your team, whatever its size or make-up, there are many counterparts of that young boy, whose fundamental motives, hungers and needs are in your own hands. You may never probe deeper than their pre-conscious hungers: you should never need to. The improvement in performance on the part of the majority of your workforce, in particular the high fliers, will come. And you will discover later on in this book why the average in terms of your overall workforce are more significant than the star performers. But before leaving the subject of psychological theory let us examine the possibility and practicality of applying it to people at work.

In the interest of brevity, the complex route from the psychologists' research findings to the practicalities of the office and shopfloor will be excluded; the interest should rest with the 'how to' approach rather with the development of the reasons why. The logic of this structure will be apparent in the eight elements which combine to create it. These eight elements are: opportunity, objectives, criteria, rules, judging, scoring, pay-off and realisation.

The parallel motivational structure

This heading begs for an obvious question, 'why parallel?' and it has an equally obvious answer. It takes a long time to incorporate these briefly outlined research results into the corporate structure of any undertaking. But results in a number of years' time – maybe a decade or more – are no good in this fiscal year. Improvements are needed on day one of an incentive campaign. Whichever way you attempt the incentives exercise, whether you use the resources of an incentive company or the assistance of this book in developing your own motivation programme, the result will be an operation which runs alongside or parallel with the long-term measures which you are planning.

As expected, the parallel motivational structur has a beginning and an end. The beginning is n less important than the end and each element in between is vitally important.

Opportunity

Always think positively when creating the incentive opportunity and everything connected with it, for that is the way to ensure that the participants think the same way. The participants should always regard the incentive programme a an opportunity to satisfy their psychological appetites, hungers and needs. This means, naturally, that the method of announcing the campaign must be the most exciting introductio available, with all the creativity which can be mustered. Everything must be positive; there is no room for penalty clauses, caveats or warnings If conditions have to be imposed, steer a positiv course. For example, if there is to be no award whatever until a qualifying performance level or 'baseline' is achieved, avoid wording such as, 'There is no award until . . . is achieved' or 'yo must reach . . . before qualifying for . . .'. Your people will react far more positively if you say: 'once you reach . . . your awards start mounting up'.

In the same way, never de-motivate by announcing an 'incentive scheme'. Select your words with care. Incentive implies that one is being 'got at', manipulated, inveigled into doing something against one's will; 'scheme' implies sinister undertones, conjuring up visions of Uria Heep and other scheming types. By all means discuss incentives among those who are used to the term, but always announce them as 'award programmes'. Do not think that you are deceiving anyone: what you are actually doing is describing your projects using positive words; like the optimist who always has a half-full glass never a half-empty one.

The opportunity you are presenting to your

participants is to acquire highly attractive and desirable benefits. It must be so; anything less is a waste of time, effort and resources. Nor are they gifts. They are awards to be earned, or won, by doing something. And the 'something' is achieving, or better still exceeding, a personal objective. One campaign will have two objectives in the minds of each participant. The one you set them and the one they set you themselves. This is where great care is needed. Set an objective higher than theirs and you have a problem. Set a slightly lower target and greater results can be achieved. However, do not be too anxious, particularly if you are making a certain award value available below the objective with far more at and above the target level. If all eight elements of your motivational structure are in place your worthwhile participants will set themselves a 'target', translated into award terms, which is surprisingly high, a target in performance terms that you might well not dare to impose. Above all, the objectives (personal, team and overall) must be realistic.

Simply stated, the criteria are the parameters within which the campaign is structured. In other words, the products, services or specific areas of activity which are featured; the benefits to those taking part and to the sponsoring company. Never try to manipulate your workforce into thinking that your company is a philanthropic charity! Spell out exactly who is eligible (it really should be everyone) and why, if it is unavoidable, some are excluded.

Rules

The perfect motivation campaign rules have yet to be written. But if we had to write them, they would comprise five words: 'Do this and win that.' Remember the simpler your rules, the fewer your rules, the fairer your rules – the better your campaign. Positive language applies just as much to the rules as to any other element of communication. One way of simplifying rule and reflecting the positive element in them is to avoid repeating words. For example, 'The detai announced elsewhere on this folder' (or whateve 'are deemed to be part of these rules'. Nothing negative about that – and space-saving too!

Another useful practice is to keep the rules to minimum and create a panel – including partic pant representation – to arbitrate on any query (never dispute) which can turn into a 'them-versus-us' situation.

Judges

Think of the number of judges at the Olympic Games. There are hundreds of them: the official the country's team, not to mention the several thousand spectators in the stadium. Casting you judgement is peer recognition taken to its ultimate, and 'mother' and 'father' images multiplie many times over. Not only are sensation hunger satisfied but the appetite for acclaim is also catered for.

Scoring system

A scoring system is vitally important. In any sporting event every competitor measures progress, and it is the same with an incentive programme. It is motivational suicide to announce the campaign on day one and then announce the results after a long gap in communication.

Scoring devices which record participants' successes to date frequently call for imaginative creativity. The league table is one way, with encouraging comments on the performances of individuals who are ahead, those coming up fast, those approaching the leaders, etc. The regular statements, produced by some incentive companies who operate an award currency 'banking system' – all these not only inform but motivat in their own right, well worth the allocation of a sizeable slice of the programme budget.

Pay-off

'Pay-off' does not mean the payment of currency or gifts to ensure that something is kept quiet. In this instance it means the opposite: while award 'currency' may well change hands, the fact that it has is shouted from the roof-tops, with all the creativity and communicational skills available. The 'fact' is all about achievement; personal, team and company achievement of 'milestone' performance levels.

When your first participants reach the target, congratulate them and tell the world! When the company achieves 50 per cent of its total quota, congratulate everyone (without going over the top) and encourage them to see the possibility of breaking the target before the end of the programme. Always look for good news to broadcast.

The climax (but not the conclusion) of this element is the end of the programme, when everything is totted up. The final awards are allocated, the names of the supreme award winners splashed across the front of the house magazine, or the bulletin sheet, for the chairman or managing director and the local manager or supervisor to add their praise and acclaim to those of the award-winning team. However, the pay-off does not end there. If there is a travel award, or an award dinner, it is photographed, written up and featured up to seven weeks after the close of the programme. A glance at the 'Time and Motive' chart on page 82 will indicate the potential effects of this publicity, even if there is no final function, merely the last instalment of the award currency. The photographs of delighted winners' families receiving, admiring and using their prizes or awards and suitable quotes from all concerned will show a return which will surprise as well as delight you!

Realisation

Although realisation is not the major element

motivation, it is the element to which everything else points, the final element all participants look forward to.

The people who receive these awards are not customers. Customers, important as they are, receive merchandise and other benefits in return for money, which they pay at the time of receipt or, hopefully, during an agreed credit period. Your people have 'paid' for the awards in skill and hard work – and in advance, too. If customers are worthy of first class service, value for money and the widest possible selection, should your workforce be given anything less?

Each of these eight elements has a place in the development of motivation programmes, therefore each must have its place in the mind of the motivator. It may sound too complex, a discipline best left to those whose profession it is. On the other hand, it may sound just the challenge you relish. Either way, whether you need to know in order to do it yourself or want to know in order to brief a specialist agency effectively, it is important to take a hard look at your own individual situation at this time and consider what application is needed.

3

To motivate or not, that is the question

Psychology is powerful material – not only did the established incentive companies enjoy a considerable boost to their morale and self-respect by learning that their policies were scientifically sound, but they seized on the newly allied disciplines in order to refine their hitherto rough-hewn approach to the market. That refinement is still going on. And you, as management in industry or commerce, can benefit from it whether you are developing your own motivation programme or preparing to brief one or more such incentive companies.

In the above statement lies one of the major pitfalls into which motivation of people at work can fall, never to rise again. It is the function, indeed the duty, of the client not only to brief the motivators and to answer all the relevant questions honestly, but to keep abreast of the programme and work closely with the agency from the start until after the finish and beyond.

The inevitable conclusion of all of this is that you, as client or motivator, need to have done preparative work long before the campaign plans are formed. One of your first questions has to be, 'Is there something we should be doing first?'

The answer depends on the climatic environment in which your intended participants work, but more importantly on who those participants are – or should be, what you want or need to achieve, and whether it is achievable. Another factor for consideration is whether the return, in terms of extra profitability, is worth the investment in motivational campaign costs. With these and other variables, plus the inherent inexactitude of 'people' sciences, it will not be surprising that our advice is, 'When in doubt, leave it out'.

Your first task should not be to find answers to all the variables and thereby eliminate them – that is patently impossible. It is to reduce the degree of doubt to an acceptable minimum. Perhaps the one factor above all that will decide whether you find the answers to the variables yourself (or from within your organisation or the professionals) is the size and the complexity of your organisation. Let us assume, therefore, that you decide to call in the professionals from an incentive company.

Professional assistance

When these professionals are called in, they will probably want to conduct research into the motivational 'temperature' of the potential participating complement of your workforce. Provided they can show you examples of previous research (although the names of their clients could be withheld due to confidentiality) and can demonstrate the logic behind their methods, you should be able to rely on their findings.

Even if there are no examples of research methods on offer, you should have the motivational agency visit the work areas, and experience the environment of typical participants. You should be able to advise them on which are comparatively good, bad and average groups to visit; incidentally, do not tell the agency which are which, just nominate the groups and leave it at that – let them do the work.

When their findings and recommendations are presented, check out the new comparisons with your own and query them if necessary. You may find a discrepancy which the agency confirms and can substantiate – this will, of course, only serve to confirm that lines of communication between management and the workforce are precisely *from* management *to* field, without the benefits of two-way communication. This in itself justifies a decision to engage an outside source to carry out research. The main difference between internal research and external research is the potential the latter provides for frankness since respondents are replying to people who are perceived as non-threatening rather than 'the bosses at head office', with possible subsequent victimisation.

It has been known that the instigation of this research has produced benefits in addition to those hoped for by introducing the possibility of a subsequent motivation programme. In one organisation, many typical responses were, 'What? Don't tell me the Head Office are actually going to listen, much less consult us!'

However, one factor is in danger of being overlooked when deciding whether or not to motivate. The danger of motivating incompetence. Do the people out there really know all they should know about how to succeed and benefit? Step back and take a fresh look. Perhaps company policy dictates, for example, that sales people are regularly up-dated on product knowledge plus order/invoice/credit procedures. And every few years or so they attend a sales refresher course at a local hotel. On the other hand, possibly other participants would not be fully aware of all that would be required of them to benefit from the programme.

Objectives and award structures

There are many other considerations which should be examined before launching an award campaign. One which must be mentioned –

although it should go without saying – is the current level of remuneration of the potential participants. If this remuneration is low and corporate well-being allows, it should be rectified to match the market and the region. To impose targets and objectives on people who are experiencing problems in meeting day to day living expenses is hardly conducive to enthusiasm, especially if the awards are luxuries. Incentive awards, of whatever form, should be in addition to an already adequate pay and benefit structure.

There is a delicate balance between positive and negative motivation. A motivation award programme, however well-designed and creatively produced, will do little to remove such negatives as poor company policy, supervision, work conditions, salary (unless the awards are to be cash, but read Chapters 5 and 7) and security. It may well have an influence upon 'relationship with peers', 'personal life' and 'status', but eliminating the dissatisfaction does not, in itself, produce positive motivation. The ratio is 19:69. Raise your eyes, and your sights, to factors such as achievement, recognition, responsibility (if only for one's own function), and advancement and you are looking at not only the factors which motivate but the stuff of which, psychologically, the kind of award programmes outlined in this book are made.

It is not surprising, in view of these logical deductions, that the eight-element structure revealed in Chapter 2 is called a 'parallel motivation structure'. Not only does it operate in parallel with long-term employee relations objectives such as job-enrichment but it follows closely the direction towards positive motivation (at least as far as conscious influences go). And as case histories will later show, the reason why the incentive business grew, flourished and is still hale and hearty today, is that it works.

The next stage is to ask yourself four fundamental questions. If the incentive agency you have brought in does not ask questions very similar to these, think twice before engaging them: unless, that is, you have done their work for them and answered the fundamental four questions in your comprehensive brief. These are:

1 What does your company want to achieve?
2 Who can influence that achievement?
3 In what time-scale do you need to achieve results?
4 What is it worth financially to guarantee achievement?

There are two temptations here, both are easy to fall into. Ask any experienced motivational agency executive how many times the answer to the first question has been 'more sales' or 'more productivity' or 'less waste' or 'fewer accidents' or a combination. These answers are not enough, not by a long way: objectives are made of more than this. First, answers must be quantified, second, answers must be realistically achievable, and thirdly – particularly if this is your first venture into motivation through incentives – research should be done in stages and kept as simple as possible.

Setting specific targets and objectives has always been something of a crystal ball operation, particularly in sales and marketing. Safety and accident prevention has only one target – no accidents at all. The same applies to waste and rejects. Production of components, assembly shop output and stock control are quantifiable to a large degree. It is not a 'get-out' to suggest, when faced with a number of objectives whose desirability does not greatly vary, that you could do a lot worse than select one which can easily be quantified *and* can be seen by the participants to have been quantified. Naturally, as everyone (including you) gets accustomed to the concept and the award structure of your first programme, those that follow can gradually become more complex. Of course, the really astute manager or incentive agency executive can perhaps spot one objective on your list which will incorporate others.

Take safety/accident prevention, for instance. Any safety officer will provide meaningful objectives in terms of lost-time accidents (man-hours) between them. There are two more worthwhile objectives hidden in that last sentence: one is absenteeism and the other is time-keeping, both concealed by the term 'lost time'.

Does it sound unusual to you to give people prizes in order to motivate them not to hurt themselves? At least four petroleum companies would respectfully disagree to the tune of several hundred thousand pounds a year each in incentive campaign budgets. The only reason they do not invest quite so much now as when they started is that motivation's most beneficial by-product, the formation of good habits instead of harmful ones, has added its influence to the award structure. Instead of attempting to reduce the lost time accidents below a factor of around 25, these companies' concern now is to keep it below three.[1] So when petroleum company A motivates people to work and drive safely in order 'To be safe, to be well, to be happy', they subconsciously add a silent, 'To be here, every day and on time'.

[1]Calculations devised by ROSPA (Royal Society for the Prevention of Accidents) in terms of accident frequency per million man-hours or per 100,000 kilometres of driving.

Some objectives totally defy calculation, particularly on an individual participant's basis. How does one measure the productivity of certain members of your workforce? How do you calculate the target for one member of a foundry team on whose performance depends that of others and vice versa? Do not even try. Instead, divide the complement into teams and award each team member on the basis of the overall performance of the team. How the team allocation is done depends on the circumstances of the campaign; sometimes it is best to use natural boundaries such as shifts, departments, etc., sometimes a random vertical slice is taken, incorporating all ranks, while the usual system comprises horizontal slice: sales people, area managers, regional managers, etc.

Paradoxically, when deciding on objectives, and doing your utmost to pin yourself down to one only, a golden opportunity may be missed or, worse still, endanger the cost-effectiveness of the campaign. A perfect example is the launch of a new product. 'Sell the new, hydrolysed brand of Foamy into every outlet!' may be the stentorian call of the motivation programme but, if that is precisely what your representatives do to the exclusion of all your other brands that are not carrying any discount, your marketing people might not share the euphoria. What you should do is involve all your company's products, with a bonus for each order over target, and an even larger bonus for hitting all product targets as well.

Continuing with our example of sales people, the following briefly covers the variations in objective(s) which normally accompanies variations in what people do. Setting targets for sales representatives is comparatively straightforward, if not actually easy; area, regional or other line managers can present other problems since their function is not merely selling – indeed, may not even involve selling at all. If an area manager sells, the objective could well be the total performance of the area against area target. What if the area manager (or regional/divisional manager) plays an extraordinary managerial role? How do you measure leadership, guidance, inspiration, motivation of the area team by their immediate supervisor? By its effect on the team, of course. Although this aspect is really part of the award structure and is covered more thoroughly later, the topic cannot be left as structure depends largely on objectives.

Consider the area managers' effect on their teams. To include them on the programme you could say, 'your target is the total of your representatives' targets'. A better way is to tell them, 'You earn (say) 140 per cent of the average award per participant in your team.' Using this method recognises the area manager's greater responsibility and higher rank.

However, the subtle and psychological motivator will go further than this. The approach to the area manager will be, 'You can earn the sum of the award to your most successful and least successful representative.' The actual award value may not appear to be any different from the average-per-representative total, but the difference in effect on the manager will be noticeable.

(a) the realisation that success depends on the team;
(b) changing the appearance of the team from an indistinct, amorphous whole into a number of separate individuals, each different from the others but needing to be led, guided, inspired, in their own way.

The experienced area manager will waste less time on the area 'stars' who will carry on doing their job, and be available to them only if assistance is needed. It is the average or below-average performers who need help at the moment and will get it. As time passes these performers will need less and less time spent on them. The manager will know it from the fact that they are no longer the 'least successful' area participants. Suddenly, others need help.

The simple objective of the area manager concerned is to lead, guide, inspire and motivate each of the team so that those who start off by being the 'least successful' award-earners finish the campaign within a whisker of the 'stars'. How can you be sure? The answer is by using the award scale. The manager's real objective is to earn as closely as possible to twice the stars' award value. Having admitted that setting targets for sales people is easier than for their managers, one must also admit that measuring non-sales, non-production functions such as administration, design, store-keeping, cleaning, hotel occupations, and so on, present problems in keeping the score. With luck, you will find answers – inspirations at least – from later examples and case studies on this topic. One thing you can be sure of, the list will never be completed. Someone, somewhere, will always add to it!

Marketing objectives for incentives

Throughout this book the need for motivational programmes to be offered to the widest spectrum of employees, wholesalers, dealers and others, has been emphasised. It is not merely the sales forces which should be the beneficiaries of such programmes. However, the following 44 points will illustrate the ramifications of the possibilities of motivational programmes as they could affect sales.

1 Increase off-season sales
2 Win new customers
3 Sell the full line
4 Introduce new products
5 Introduce new models
6 Counter competitors' promotion
7 Reduce overstocking
8 Increase sales calls
9 Install dealer displays
10 Promote special deals
11 Build sales enthusiasm
12 Open new outlets
13 Increase factory production
14 Reduce absenteeism or lateness
15 Improve work habits
16 Reduce training time
17 Cut down on waste
18 Improve customer service
19 Increase demonstrations
20 Encourage volume buying
21 Increase proposals and presentations
22 Qualify prospects

23 Step up production
24 Secure new or more leads
25 Recruit new employees
26 Re-activate former accounts
27 Get journey reports in on time
28 Increase tie-in sales
29 Reduce order processing costs
30 Lower the accident rate
31 Lower the claims or damage rate
32 Encourage service personnel to sell
33 Increase distributor stocking
34 Increase dealer stocking
35 Stimulate step-up selling
36 Increase number of orders per customer
37 Encourage prompt, accurate reports
38 Encourage customer leads to new prospects
39 Improve sales representatives' attitudes
40 Develop new uses for products
41 Increase sales of slow movers
42 Smooth out production curve
43 Obtain reports or leads produced by advertising
44 Close sales after proposals are made

4 Budgeting, how much should a programme cost?

The inclusion of a chapter on how to fund a motivational programme, in advance of five other chapters about structuring the operation, demonstrates the important aspects of this approach to the subject.

1 Money is the first consideration when deciding what to do about objectives which must be achieved.
2 The level of the available funding may well decide, or at least materially influence, the type and complexity of the award structure around which the programme is constructed.

You will notice that these two aspects are stated as being those that prevail; however, whether or not they should is another matter, since the four fundamental questions which the motivator asks are:

(a) What is the objective (are the objectives)?
(b) Who can influence achievement?
(c) When is the optimum time and period?
(d) What is it worth to achieve your objective(s)?

The question of cost plainly comes last, and is

expressed in terms of benefit rather than budget; the answers to those previous four questions dictate the monetary investment in an incentive programme. 'How much can we afford to spend?' While some campaigns, entered into by management on this basis, do succeed in achieving their stated objective, many more fail miserably. The reason is both simple and obvious – management attitude.

It is not putting it too strongly to say that many incentive campaigns fail because the first people who must be motivated are not. And remember the opposite of motivation is not demotivation but non-motivation. The rule must be: management must be motivated first, and at least as much as the campaign participants will need to be! The attitude of management to the subject of incentive programme budgets has got to be positive – and that fact must be obvious throughout the programme and across the participant spectrum.

Award-winning opportunities

If it is admitted that the objective is the first consideration, what follows in natural sequence? If you have read Chapter 2 you will know the answer – opportunity. This progression highlights the need to provide a worthwhile award-winning opportunity (AWO) for each participant who achieves improvement in performance, whatever the budget may appear to be. Hence, from the total campaign budget available, a large proportion should be reserved for actual, tangible reward. Leave a reserve amount for the announcement or launch, a proportion for the follow-up materials, another sum for a proper, efficient administration system and an allocation for the requirements of the Inland Revenue.

Before deciding where the money is to come from one must first discover, at least to 'ballpark' accuracy, what level of AWO will achieve the incentive campaign's objective.

A reasonable starting point is the current level of remuneration that each person enjoys in total, including wages and all other benefits that go with the job as well as commissions and bonuses. Nor is it functionable or workable to take away part of your employees' total remuneration, giving it a coat of 'incentive-coloured' paint and returning it to them provided they achieve the objective. Some material benefit, in addition to existing cash and perks, must be offered because effort and results, in addition to existing performance, are being called for.

The prime budgetary consideration, therefore, is not whether an extra budget needs to be found but where the money is to come from. In principle, the budget comes from part of the extra profit that is the subject of this book.

It should now be clear why 'budget' should always follow 'objectives' in the mind of the motivator. If one can discover the actual value of the answer to (d) on page 33 the potential budget has been located. Many incentive campaign budgets are – literally – hard to find. They exist, of that there is no doubt, but many are cunningly concealed. For instance, take the distribution network that was losing money on pallets used for delivery of goods. Half or fewer of these pallets were being returned. How does a transport manager squeeze money out of the board of directors for an incentive campaign to reduce pallet loss? The manager in this case duly cancelled an order for the next 100 pallets and used a proportion of the savings to mount an incentive campaign. The campaign paid out an award currency value of 50p per existing pallet brought back in good condition. Let us assume the cost of new pallets to be £20 each. Assume also that the average pallet's life is perhaps eight return journeys. If all pallets come back immediately after use the per pallet delivery becomes £2.50. Suddenly, pallets by the score appeared as if by magic. Pallet life went from eight round trips to over forty. Delivery drivers and their families started to enjoy choosing and using the fruits of the incentive campaign. And this incentive campaign is still in force today.

However, it is more often than not the task of the motivator to find, or at least to justify, expenditure from one source or another for an incentive programme. This can be a daunting task – and for powerful and understandable reasons. Every pound takes funds which could be used for research and development, expansion, new equipment, expansion of corporate services, etcetera. Labour costs, of course, feature large in boardroom deliberations, particularly in the wake of the swing to a service industry economy, and what are incentive campaigns but a sizeable increase in those very costs. 'Spend the money on technology to replace labour' is the cry from senior executives.

What do they really mean? They may say that this kind of expense, usually labelled 'marketing costs', offers an unacceptably less tangible, less measurable, return on investment. For the phrase 'less tangible' read 'outside our normal sphere of experience', for 'less measureable' read 'it might work too well'.

One ideal place for such stimulating campaign structures is the clearance of one product to maximise the impact of a new model launch. Once the products have gone, they have gone; so the maximum budget is easy to calculate, particularly on a straight remuneration of 'x' award currency per unit sold.

One major motor manufacturer in the UK exploited this to great effect some years ago, by offering every dealer's sales representatives incentive currency per model sold retail before the launch date of model 10 weeks later. Over 90,000 certified retail sales were made in the weeks; the sponsor even diverted units destined for export to cope with the demand created by the participants. The cost of this incentive campaign was less than one-seventieth of its advertising budget for that year. So how do you justify the cost?

Marginal cost vs profit

In simple terms, this means you gain in proportion to what you spend. Virtually every incentive programme has both fixed and variable cost elements. Fixed costs include computer time, promotional materials, launch meetings, etc, plus the professional's fee if that is incurred. These are spent whatever happens. Variable costs are largely dependent on awards – which in turn are dependent on results. Profit, on the other hand, is entirely variable – it starts at zero.

Mathematics demonstrate that there is a 'break-even' point where profit (incremental or marginal) on motivated sales exactly covers the combined fixed and variable costs up to that point. If sales exceed this figure the programme more than covers its cost. Therefore, you should graphically as well as with figures demonstrate the achievability of that break-even point and the effect of over/under-achievement. It should also anticipate the impact of a price cut by your competitors in their like-product range.

Return on investment

This method starts off just like the first one, but you also add in the timing of cash inflow and outflow. A typical incentive programme has an initial outflow (the fixed costs, mainly), followed by inflow from sales, then increased inflow from the projects – whose benefits accrue long after the investment – with motivation programme money spent largely post-benefit.

Zero-based budgeting

Each activity, irrespective of its initial cost or what increase that cost shows year by year, is judged on its merits. What you do is break down the department's function into logical activity groups, then each group of activities into various levels, calculating a cost/benefit rate for each. Then, having decided the best way of achieving each objective activity level and where each level comes in order of importance and cost-effectiveness, you select the number of projects to be given the green light until the funds are all allocated. Judged against all three criteria if your programme has a high score it should feature high on 'funding' priority – provided that its structure, its objectives and its award pay-out are viable and of sufficient power.

Let us say that you have 40 sales people, eight area supervisors and two regional sales managers; it is agreed that a three-month campaign is indicated. First, consider the award value to offer those at the 'sharp end', the 40 'sales people'. No-one really knows who first propounded 7.5 to 10 per cent of total earnings as a good working award basis for sales people's incentive campaigns. This percentage relates to merchandise or merchandise/travel as awards not cash or recognition symbols; the fine difference between these terms is dealt with in the following chapters. Assume for our example, however, that merchandise is to be the main award.

A sales representative's total earnings (not remuneration) can range widely. Assume each representative earns £10,000 per annum. The award value offered for target achievement, therefore, is 7.5 to 10 per cent of £2,500 over three months which is between £187.50 and £250. The earnings of area supervisors and regional sales managers will not be examined: their awards will depend on the success of the representative under their control, as Chapter 3 indicated, and their awards will be:

Supervisors
Each area supervisor receives the sum of the award value earned by the most and least successful representative in the area.

Regional sales managers
Each receives the sum of the award value earned by the most and least successful area supervisor in the region.

Creating an award budget

Now we can start calculating our representative equivalent, a useful figure on which to base our budget.

Representatives:	40 × £200	£8,000

Area supervisors, assuming all representatives in the area hit the target, each area supervisor therefore earns twice a representative's award value.

Representative's equivalent is:

	2 × 8 × £200	£3,200

Area sales managers, assuming that both earn twice as much as area supervisors' award value.

Representative equivalent is:

	2 × 4 × £800	£1,600
Theoretical total award budget		£12,800

Figure 2 overleaf shows that each representative reaches 50 per cent of target before 20 per cent of target award is earned. At 75 per cent the award is 30 per cent of the total. By the time 60 per cent of target award is paid out, at least 90 per cent of target has been achieved. And 'target' is usually well over normally expected output.

There are only two more variables to consider: target levels and over-target award values. Target levels is the one function of motivation in which you are on your own when it comes to viability. Whether the ideal motivation results in a viable outlay per unit sold overall is something only you and your colleagues can say. To work out your target level and award value levels ask yourself the following questions.

Fig 2: On-target award value

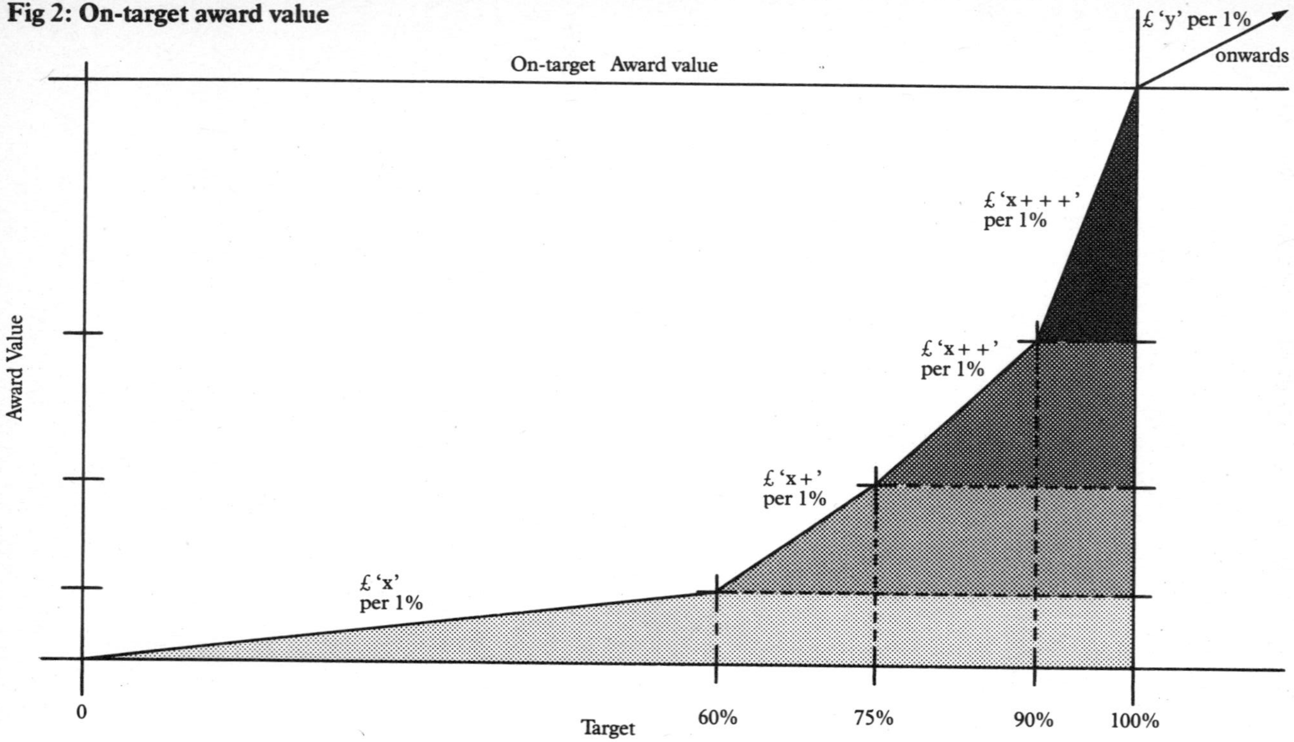

1 What proportion of the representatives will beat target?
2 By how much will they beat target?
3 What effect will those two answers have on the total company achievement with regard to target?

Once you have answered these three questions there is one further consideration. Not a variable this time, but something that affects your campaign budget more than any other single influence – income tax. Income tax is payable on all 'benefits in kind' including incentive benefits. This is an important consideration, but more on that subject in Chapter 10.

There are several kinds of budgeting methods too: negative objectives (reducing accidents, eliminating clerical errors, etc). The tendency when evaluating budgets is to count the cost of accidents in man-hours lost, multiplied by hourly pay in the time it takes to correct errors. Nothing could be wider of the mark. Accident and errors cost much more than man-hours lost. Lost materials and flagging morale are just a few areas affected.

Base-line budget

One excellent award scale is to allocate an award per achievement level reached. When doing so, base the target on what at least half the complement could achieve with the extra impetus of the campaign. For example, suppose the three-month 'norm' for sales for Foamy is 10,000 units per representative, and if the next three months were to turn over 15,000 units, you could afford, say, 45p per unit. When the representative hits the base line, he receives a bonus of 15p per unit sold so far. And from base line up to target the award remains at 30p per unit. However, from target upward (as target is a hefty slice above the 'norm') the award payout is three times the 'base line' award. From start of base line your output or payout is virtually nil. From 'norm' to target the award per 1 per cent is at least reasonable, while from there upwards the increase is noticeable indeed.

Up to base line	100 award points per case
Base line to target	200 award points per case

On target, a bonus of award points to bring your total up to

300 award points per case

And 300 points a case thereafter.

In all cases the first consideration is achieving the objective and the second is doing so profitably.

The 'points a case' award method can, of course, be applied not only to your own employees but to those of your wholesalers, dealers, retailers, etc – and very effectively too. But if you really want to bring out the best in your dealer personnel over a long period you must include the dealer proprietor/managing director/partners/chairman – the overall term is 'dealer principal'.

'Earn-back'

Earn-back is a most effective method of offering considerable award values, such as magnificent group incentive travel to your distributors – and (if necessary) the award to their personnel – with a very much reduced or eliminated risk of overbudgeting. It also allows all dealerships and their principals to benefit, despite the large numbers of them which you might have. The earn-back advantages are described further in Chapter 6 but the principle, like so many aspects of motivation campaigns, greatly affects the question of budgets.

Perhaps you have so many dealers to offer group incentive travel (costing you something like £1,000 per head – £2,000 per dealership) that without earn-back you cannot justify taking them all. So you offer them all a place for two on the following terms:

Achievement	*You will fund*
80 per cent of dealership target	Half the cost of one person
100 per cent of dealership target	The total cost of one person
120 per cent of dealership target	The total cost of one person plus half the cost of the other

Each dealership either pays the total two person cost up front or, more usually, commits itself to total payment on or before departure. Corresponding reservations can be made and considerable savings are possible. Your benefit is that you know from day one that your investment is covered.

The commitment from you – the incentive motivator – should be to generate budgets that will enhance your campaign results which, in turn, will lead to greater profitability. Do not overcost but on the other hand it is worth remembering that you can rarely 'get something for nothing'.

5

Which incentive award will work best for you?

The most significant and relevant way in which to begin this chapter on matching your award to your participants is with the end. The end, that is, of the heading in the list of contents: which incentive award will work best for you? Those last two words are the operative ones. They convey the real, overwhelming, fundamental reason for motivating people at work, which is *profit*.

In order to achieve this profit you have to motivate your employees and that means finding the right method to use. You will already have found out that what motivates one person will leave another cold. This applies not only to actual awards – the catalogue items, the cup, trophy or medal of honour, the holiday for two, and so on – but to the method by which your participants obtain them. If you give them the money, what will they buy with it? Which store vouchers give the widest choice and best reflect the kind of person who received them? If there was one answer for *each* of your participants all the time, things might be simpler, but each individual is just that and so things are not that simple. A new version of Abraham Lincoln's adage, about fooling some of the people some of

the time, applies to incentive awards and award media with at least equal force.

It helps if you consider who, as well as what, your participants are. If you are running a sales campaign, should it be for those out at the sharp end only or the line management as well? Or perhaps you should encourage regional/district managers to inspire and drill their representatives to do what they were hired for and trained for and are paid for.

A little thought will resolve this query. You will remember the segregation of performance levels in Chapter 2: 7.5 per cent to 10 per cent of high fliers, 80 per cent or so of average performers and 7.5 per cent to 10 per cent 'in transit'. It should go without saying that as job roles differ and people's performances within these different job categories, so too must remuneration differ. It makes sense, therefore, to create a common bond between all ranks no matter where they are placed in your organisation. Hence the sales force, the team, the shift, the department, should all be motivated – granted in different ways – so that all should be pulling together for your company's benefit. This means cooperation from the management depending on sales staff all the way up to and including your head office. Do not miss out *anyone* who can influence the achievement of objectives.

The point at which to stop adding names to the participants' list is when, in spite of all the advice and comments in the previous chapter, the budget just will not accept anyone else without jeopardising the results and awards for everyone. It is obviously good planning and budgeting on your part if that point coincides with the bottom of the participants' list.

A case in point

A well-known insurance company in the North of England ran a sales campaign for their 2,300 sales agents with two objectives. First, they wanted to increase the net policies with premiun payments weekly in '*Industrial Branch*', the tradi tional weekly call by insurance men and the regular entry of payments in their blue books an second, they wanted to maximise the monthly, quarterly and annual policy sales in '*Ordinary Branch*', whose premiums are frequently paid by direct debit.

So successful was the sales incentive campaign that the poor bewildered staff in 260 district offices, overwhelmed with extra work, began making errors in the documentation that flooded through their hands en route to the head office. This was a serious situation, not only in duplication of effort but in customer relations. The person in charge of incentive company motivation, who had developed the agents' campaign, suggested that all branch office staff receive 'prize points' depending on how low their error rate per person per month. This was to be recorded by return of documents by the head office for correction.

The wisdom of adding district office staff to the list of campaign participants (with their own scale, of course) was borne out when inside six months the error rate per office participant went down to one- third of what it had been before the agents sales campaign began!

These factual examples are simple but they go to demonstrate what can be achieved at every level. The key is the matching of the right incentive medium to the right participants. You woulc not, of course, expect to motivate the Alpha Brewery sales force with Omega Wines vouchers but, on a different level altogether, lorry drivers and maintenance crews might not be impressed by the opportunity to push themselves to the limi in return for a collection of hand-embroidered doyleys – no matter how exquisite their appearance. Similarly, dealer principals are not going to get over-enthusiastic when they hear that the award is a week in a 'singles' fun resort.

Perhaps the worst example of mismatching awards to participants was a well-known car manufacturer who decided to run an 'incentive programme' in which all the staff, throughout the plant, who achieved production targets would go into a draw for a currently manufactured model. The crunch in this mismatched campaign came when the model was withdrawn due to difficulties!

By now the importance of using psychological hungers in the motivation of the individuals in your work force should have been recognised as the first step towards creating the desire to achieve.

Now is the turn of research. Examining and matching the best suited items of merchandise, travel destinations and recognition symbols to the appropriate participant level is a complex task. Therefore, it is important to ask two basic questions when structuring a motivation campaign – especially to the second and third.

1 Who can achieve the campaign objective?
2 How much is it worth to achieve the objectives?

The answer to the second question determines the participants and careful research must then be carried out to arrive at the type of award which provides the all important stimulus and enthusiasm. A major factor will be establishing the income groups and socio-economic status of the various levels of participants and to ensure the awards offered will ensure the achievement of the necessary goals.

Having established the type of awards necessary to be included in the campaign, the selection and purchasing of these can be facilitated by visiting the many exhibitions that are regularly staged. However, do remember that each company exhibiting products or services will probably include a degree of bias in their favour in what they say.

Your individual research should have offered up a list of suitable merchandise for each category within your workforce. But here are a few examples. Suppose you are motivating your wholesalers, dealers and distributors to sell more of your products. Why not broach the subject of a part funding by the dealership. Add that for every £10 they put in, you will put in a further £5 or £10 or even £20. After all, you are helping to improve their personnel's performance for their business.

In the same incentive programme, why not add a further strategy to include product knowledge and sales talk technique quizzes. Include point-of-sale display competitions at your dealers' premises, and remind your opposite number in the advertising department that, not only are you increasing the deployment of their materials, but for a contribution you can supply valuable market research information. You will be surprised at th willing attitude when you involve others in your campaign. Attitude, benefit and presentation are key components here.

Are you running a sales incentive campaign? Put in a call planning element in your programme to reduce mileage (and time) between selling opportunities. Not only will you get more calls per day without ever mentioning it, but the company cars will benefit. Which is good news for fleet management, and perhaps you can coax a little from their coffers!

In order to encourage employee involvement in a motivation programme, some sponsors, particularly banks and insurance companies, will encourage their non-sales employees to try and obtain extra business for their company. It may at first appear to be difficult to persuade the average bank employee to go out and sell the bank's services. However, in many cases this has been very tactfully and cleverly achieved by introducing a programme using the theme of 'Tell-a-Friend'. And with certain constraints and adjustments, this programme may help you.

The programme operates with each member of

staff being issued with a book of introductory cards. At specially arranged training meetings the employees are instructed how to use these introductory cards when handing them out to their friends and relatives. The contact approach can be made at any social gathering, a tennis club or sports club. The conversation may start something like this, 'Are you happy with the services you are getting at your particular bank? If not, and you feel you would benefit from it, why don't you go and see Mr X, the manager at our High Street branch and hand in this card. I have signed it and I can assure you that should you want information and advice on the services offered, Mr X will be very pleased to meet you and offer all the help and assistance you may require.' When the friend indicates that he or she would like to follow through on the introduction offer, the employee simply enters the name of the contact on one side and says, 'Simply go to the bank, hand this in and you will receive very special attention from the manager.'

This approach does not give the impression of the employee actually *selling* the bank's services. On the other hand, it did enhance the employee's stature in the eyes of his friend because it was felt that his friend – the bank's employee – was someone of importance and had the authority to arrange such a meeting. The introductory card was numbered and the contact would then visit the manager at the local branch. Being aware of the existence of the campaign, the manager would immediately arrange to see the contact and then provide him with the advice required. If the contact opened any type of account or used any of the services provided, the employee who initiated the introduction would earn prize points relating to the value of the business produced as indicated on the schedule of awards.

At the same time the programme also provided a basic training programme for all employees motivating them to keep the bank's interest foremost in their thoughts. Other than the campaign structure, the training structure included handing cards to all employees asking questions such as:

(a) What is the minimum amount of money which is required to open a current account?
(b) What is the minimum amount of money which is required to open a deposit account?
(c) Which of our accounts pays the top rate of interest?
(d) How long can a customer keep travellers' cheques before they are invalid?

The answers were noted on the reverse of the card, so it was simplicity itself for the employees to complete the card correctly and send it to the campaign headquarters. Each card submitted qualified for a small prize point award which provided a 'fast start' opportunity together with the creation of a great degree of initial interest in the subsequent activity. Funding for this section of the programme was provided, justifiably, from the bank's training budget.

In establishing the schedule of awards, non-contact staff members – the 'back room' staff who rarely had contact with prospects or clients – were awarded four points for a specific achievement, the non-contact departmental managers were awarded three for that achievement. The contact staff members (tellers, cashiers, etcetera) were awarded two points and their contact managers received one point. This provided everyone with an equitable earning situation, based on their selling opportunities, both in and outside of normal banking hours.

But what if you wish to use smaller items such as diaries? And do these so-called business gifts have any motivational worth?

Business gifts

Business gifts of the pen, lighter, diary or key ring variety cannot be considered in the context of motivating through incentives. They can, at best, be classified as advertising novelties, and in themselves would certainly not inspire or motivate anyone to do anything. However, the value and type of business gift will often bear relationship to the commercial importance of the goal which you are trying to achieve.

Many companies recognise their most important customers by presenting them with, say, superb hampers costing £80 to £100 each or cases of wine of equivalent value at Christmas time. This gift is an expression of thanks for the business previously given and is coupled with the hope of receiving continued business for the coming year.

Unfortunately, many genuine gestures of this type have been misinterpreted, indeed they have been considered at times to be a bribe, to the extent that a great number of the larger corporations have issued strict instructions to their suppliers that no gifts of any nature should be offered to their buyers. Others have stipulated that any gift should not exceed, say, £10 in value. Your own company may have similar rules or specific guidelines.

It is sometimes difficult to draw the fine line which establishes whether an item is seen as a business gift or as an incentive award. The best definition which can be given is that the incentive award is seen as something which has been earned as a result of attaining a specific goal, while a gift – often an unsolicited item – is more often than not made with the hope and anticipation of unspecified business for the future.

The rule should be that a clear differentiation must be made and that the smaller items such as pens should be kept strictly for promotional work alone.

PRINCIPALITY OF MONACO
MONTE CARLO
A dream come true
MORE !
Up to now, the incentive trip has always been a form of reward. Which brings us to the question : is an incentive trip to Monte-Carlo really a reward?
Well, you'll be taking your guests to one of the loveliest destinations on the Mediterranean. A place that's overflowing with tradition, culture, history. Somewhere that's absolutely special, with a climate and scenery made in heaven.
Your guests will be welcomed in the style that Monte-Carlo is famous for – in other words, they'll be treated like royalty. Everything is designed for their pleasure, comfort and relaxation : some of the best sports facilities in Europe, fabulous shops and restaurants, festivals, galas... and a thousand other unusual, fun things to enjoy.
Is this really the way to reward outstanding results? Or a cruel temptation? Remember, your guests will never have time to see and do it all!
We'll leave you to do the explaining.
After all, they'll always have another chance to come back to Monte-Carlo.
For full information, please contact :
Direction du Tourisme et des Congrès MC 98030 Monaco Cedex. Tél. : 93 30 87 01.
Telex : 469 760 MC
or Monaco Government Tourist and Convention Office, 25 Whitehall, London SW1A 2Bs.
Tel. : 019304699. Telex : 889130 PPLUS.
Place St. Nicolas.
Gala evening in Monte Carlo
Mont-Agel Golf Club overlooking the sea.
Ogilvy & Mather
OF THE WORLD'S PRINCIPAL RESORTS
THERE IS BUT ONE PRINCIPALITY

6 Campaign structures

There is a golden rule for motivation campaign structures. Every participant should be able to benefit from the campaign, directly related to his/her contribution to its success in terms of effort, results and improvement in performance.

Why should that be the golden rule? And what is so golden about it? Simply this, any 'incentive programme' which departs from it is not a true motivational campaign structure. First, the structure would be incomplete if all did not have an opportunity to benefit. It becomes not a campaign but a contest, with your employees winners and losers. And when was the chance of being a loser a source of motivation? This aspect will be covered more thoroughly in Chapter 7 but its importance is already apparent here.

Second, the structure may be complete but if the winning or earning of awards is not directly related to the amount of effort, level of results and degree of improvement in performance, motivation is haphazard and drastically impaired, and the structure collapses.

Having defined the golden rule, therefore, it makes sense to examine a few of the more frequently used structures and to judge their effectiveness. Award values not only increase but accelerate with continued progress. Award expenditure is committed right from the beginning, from the very first percentage of the target reached, whether in sales, miles of accident-free driving, weeks of scrap-free production, whatever. But notice how little of your budget is expended before the structure begins to be profitable for the company. It can also be reassuring particularly if planning a campaign for the first time. Natural prowess, enthusiasm, drive and even an element of luck may result in one or two of your 7.5 to 10 per cent top performers achieving earlier than was expected.

Another important consideration when using the target consideration structure is that very little reward takes place until your sales begin to attract much greater unit profit by being free of fixed overheads or, for example, until you receive the benefits of reductions in your fleet premiums or until you save a complete batch of materials by substantially reducing your wasting factor. It is truly a classic award structure, and the pattern on which dozens more can be moulded.

The next structure is even more simple: 'x' award points per unit sold, from start to finish of the programme. Try it when you are launching a new product or service, or seeking distribution. For each unit read a job completed on time and on cost.

The rules are:

(a) start your units at a base level, 'x';
(b) define your final target, 'y';
(c) define each stage target, 'z';
(d) for each stage target achieved, 'n' is received.

You will not need a 'campaign committee' to adjudicate on the ambiguities of this structure!

Yet a further variation:

(a) set an award value per unit reached;
(b) define a target level;
(c) not only does each participant gain an award

value when the target is hit but if it is done within a set period of time, the value to be won is doubled;

(d) set still higher targets and treble the value upon the attainments.

Does this sound to be overgenerous? Consider what the initial cost factor really is: one-third of what you could award on the 'points-per-unit' structure which preceded it! Two-thirds of budget is being withheld until you are sure of success.

Campaigns to reduce accidents and lost man-hours

One would have thought that personal safety would be uppermost in most people's minds. However, a number of years ago incentive programmes were introduced into the US to motivate truck drivers to try to reduce their accident rate. For example, many accidents occurred when drivers reversed into loading bays, damaging not only their truck but also any unfortunate people who might have been standing there awaiting the delivery. Drivers were given prize points per month for each month where no accidents were recorded, the number of points escalating from one month to another.

Another example of incentives working to improve safety

Even if you have a sizeable budget for accident prevention incentives; even if your current record is one lost-time accident per 100 employees per week, how can you powerfully motivate them to reduce accidents and time lost from work? And how can you restrict expenses when someone (as can happen) does have an injury, say, three months into the campaign? The simplest way to illustrate this is by using an example from the oil industry. The campaign was launched on 1 March, and ran for a year. Participants were allocated to teams of 15 to 20 people. Awards were team-based – individual awards, that is, but dependent on team performance. This is how the award structure was illustrated in the launch folder.

Table 1. Award winning for each accident-free month

Month	1 No. of points	2	3	4	5	6	7	8	9	10	11	12
Month's award	100	100	100	200	200	200	300	400	500	600	800	1000
3-month bonus	—	—	300	—	—	600	—	—	1000	—	—	3000
Total for month	100	100	400	200	200	800	300	400	1500	600	800	4000
Total so far	100	200	600	800	1000	1800	2100	2500	4000	4600	5400	9400

If your team sustains a lost-time accident all you lose is that month's awards. Then, in your next accident-free month, you immediately start winning again from the Month 1 rate. There is no indication of a negative statement. Look at that award scale. The award value increases with achievement month by month, until much greater value as the objective (an accident-free team year) is reached. That is quite close to the classic 'theoretical curve'.

Rely on your research to indicate the suitability and motivational pull of the award value on a quarterly and annual basis.

Finally, consider what happens throughout your organisation.

1 Awareness of potential and existing hazards.
2 Insistence from the shop floor upwards on their removal.
3 Abolition of dangerous practices.
4 Mutual improvement and *esprit de corps*.
5 Accident reduction.

This campaign visibly improves employee and industrial relations: management and managed find themselves talking the same language to each other.

Perhaps you really are not able to extract sufficient funds to provide the necessary budget for a conventional 'campaign' award structure. Then the next best thing would be to run a contest, especially if you can make sure that the star performers do not scoop the pool each time.

But what about a combination of both? The classic 'target' awards and the simple 'points per unit'. Announce a simplified award, growing towards a given target, based on 'x' points per unit of achievement and further points once the target has been exceeded. This is useful for people you do not employ, such as wholesalers and dealers. Those smaller dealers who, on points per unit, could not hope for a very high award value, will benefit more from the classic scale. On the other hand, the larger dealers will enjoy the straight pay-out, since their throughput and therefore their targets will be much higher.

The benefit to your company would be first, the bulk of awards directed to the dealers who do the bulk of your trade and second, every dealership is motivated including the up-and-coming outlets.

As you can see, award structures are legion and there is often a temptation to introduce a new one each time you launch a motivation programme. Resist it, at least until you have a structure that proves effective. Introduce new facets by all means, but in the creative aspect rather than in the overall structure.

Ideas for dealer awards

For the most part, the motivation of employees has been covered with only a brief mention of dealer principal awards. To examine dealer awards in more detail, an example of a company's programme will be used.

The objectives of the ABC Electronics were:

(a) protect, maintain and increase the sales of its products;
(b) boost dealership morale by improving goodwill;
(c) recognise their importance to the business and isolate them from competitive threats.

After examining every possible solution, it was decided to introduce a motivation programme by offering all dealers in the 'highpower' electrical dealer network the opportunity of participating in and earning an exciting, specially designed, travel award programme. With this in mind and estimating the utilisation of the earn-back concept, and the impact it would have on future sales profits, a campaign target was calculated for each dealer. This was based on previous sales and on future sales potential. A summary of these targets revealed that projected overall sales increases would produce sufficient extra profit to provide a campaign budget of £200,000. It was also estimated that approximately 100 of the dealers would reach and exceed their individual targets and would therefore qualify for inclusion in the travel award plan. Each plan would cost £1,000 per person.

However, investigations revealed that if the numbers qualifying were to be increased and if firm reservations could be made nine months ahead of time, then this cost factor could be reduced to around £900 per person. The sponsors were also notified that the overall content of the package would have a perceived normal retail value of approximately £1,200, and even then, not all its contents could be included or provided for the individual traveller.

The dealers were then invited to attend a series of specially convened regional meetings which included an announcement of the travel award opportunity. Special care was taken to create a destination atmosphere at each venue – air hostesses in attendance, video film of the hotels, facilities and surroundings, etc., to instill a high degree of mystery and growing excitement. Then followed a lunch comprising a typical menu from the destination, after which the dealers reassembled to learn more of the incentive activity planned for them.

Dealers were encouraged to participate in and capitalise on this offer which would show them a saving of £400 per couple. Then came the announcement of the award-winning opportunities open to all dealers. Each was given a campaign target for the six months' duration of the programme. They were required to commit themselves to full participation in the programme by paying £1,000 per person at the outset of activities. In the final analysis of 190 of the 250 dealers – and their partners – elected to enrol. This produced a total promised funding of:

$$190 \times 2 \times £1,000 = £380,000$$

The table below shows the rate of achievement this dealer programme produced.

Table 2. Rate of achievement

No. of dealers	What they achieved	What each received	What the sponsoring company reimbursed
25	Failed to reach 80% of target	Nil	Nil
30	80% of target (up to 99%)	50% of £1,000	£15,000
75	100% of target (up to 119%)	100% of £1,000	£75,000
30	120% of target (up to 39%)	100% of £1,000 plus 50% of £1,000	£45,000
30	140% of target (or more)	100% of £2,000	£60,000
190			£195,000

Note: For ease of calculation, income tax requirements have not been considered.

The balance sheet of the programme is well worth looking at.

Payments guaranteed from dealerships (190 × 2 × £1,000)	£380,000
Total reimbursements to dealerships	£195,000
Balance in hand	£185,000
Cost of travel awards reserved (190 × 2 × £900)	£342,000
Deduct balance in hand	£185,000
Net cost to sponsoring company:	£157,000

The financial gains are, of course, the tangible gains – the immediate gains. Who can put a finite value on the medium and long-term benefits of gathering together 75 per cent of the dealer network in the most congenial of atmospheres?

Yet another dealer incentive programme is one called 'square deal'. Let us examine each type of participant in order.

Sales representatives: Each has been given an all-product campaign and sales target and a 'points per case' award scale. Here are the structures.

Sales of all products

For each 1 per cent of target between 50 and 80 per cent = 'x' points
For each 1 per cent between 81 and 100 per cent = 2 'x' points
For each 1 per cent over 100 per cent = 4 'x' points
For each case sold = 'y' points

Wholesalers
For each case purchased = 'z' points

The wholesalers agreed, as a condition of participation, to distribute at least half these points to their own sales force. Each wholesaler's enrolled representative was given a 'square deal' card resembling the one shown below.

Table 3. 'Square deal' card

'Full house' (All nine squares crossed out)	200 Cases of Product 'A'	150 Cases of Product 'B'	75 Sacks of Product 'C'	This row full pays 1,000
pays	4/10 Pallets of Product 'D'	9/100 Cases of Product 'Y'	5/15 Drums of Product 'E'	This row full pays 1,500 points
16,000 points in all!	6/100 Litres of Product 'F'	7/3 Tonnes of Product 'G'	8/20 Points of sale displays for all products	This row full pays 1,000
Diagonal row full 4,000 points	This row full pays 1,200 points	This row full pays 2,000 points	This row full pays 1,000 points	Diagonal row full 3,000 points

Note: As soon as a square's criteria has been met, the square is crossed off. An award is not earned until a row of three squares is crossed. Squares 1, 3, 6 and 8 are of lesser importance on a profit or priority basis, than squares 2, 4, 5 and 7. Product 'Y' is the product of prime importance. As the days go by, squares begin to be crossed out. Each representative's objective is to gain the best value rows, the most rows or all rows.

There is, of course, available space on each 'Bingo Card' for the wholesaler's validation that their representative has indeed qualified for the award value claimed.

Campaign planning

From receipt and checking-in of raw materials, through production, quality control, packing, despatch and sales right to end users, motivation can be applied. But now on to campaign planning, pulling together all the elements which are needed to ensure success. Again, another company is used as an example.

The Fastwheel Motor Corporation retails approximately 250,000 units per year throughout their 650 dealership networks. In March the decision was made to introduce a new product range to be launched and aggressively marked on 1 September next. There is already speculation as to the design and performance of the new vehicle; dealer sales/representatives are encountering resistance from prospective buyers of the current range.

Statistics reveal that as of 1 April 75,000 of the current model range will need to be sold between that date and 31 August to ensure dealerships are clear to receive the new models. The 'New Year' August registration opportunity will provide some assistance to the summer selling effort. The decision is taken to structure a motivational programme designed to sell all current stock by 5 August. An overall appropriation of £25 per unit is approved. This is broken down as follows: £15 per unit to develop a motivation programme for dealer sales managers and dealer sales representative and £10 per unit for a dealer principal campaign.

The objective is clear, and the available campaign budget is agreed at £750,000. Furthermore, it was management's express desire that all dealers, regardless of size or potential, should have a realistic opportunity of qualifying for any award plan devised for the programme. For general morale and other corporate reasons it was also decided that the award would be a VIP luxury travel award programme. In addition, each winning dealer would be accompanied by his partner. The following criteria was established and agreed upon.

Campaign period:	1 April to 5 August
	£
Gross budget: (75,000 × £10)	750,000
Provision for income tax (30 per cent of net award budget)	165,000
Reserve for promotion administration	35,000
Net award budget	550,000

The approved net budget of £550,000 would permit 100 winning dealers and their partners to qualify at a cost of £2,500 per head. Ten per cent of the budget would cover the cost for accompanying company hosts plus a contingency reserve fund. The outcome, therefore, represented a winner/participant ratio of 100/650, which was determined as being sufficient incentive for the programme to attain the desired results. The campaign, 'Set Sail for Nassau', was under way.

To ensure that all dealers received an equal opportunity, the campaign organiser placed dealers in one of four leagues, each representing a different level of their annual sales potential, as the following table shows. Each league was given a title for subsequent promotional activity. The top dealers in each league would qualify for an award.

Table 4. Set sail for Nassau

League	**The Schooners**	**The Windjammers**	**The Galleons**	**The Yachts**	**Total**
Dealers' annual contracted	Over 400 units	310–400 units	210–300 units	Less than 200 units	—
No. of dealers in league	100	300	170	80	650
No. of awards per league	20	45	25	10	100
Percentage of awards to dealers in league	20	15	14.7	12.5	15.3

Campaign announcement

In mid-March a special mailing shot was directed to all dealer principals comprising of a small toy yacht with 'Let's sale and win' imprinted on the main sail. A few days later this was followed by a postcard signed by the manager of the selected hotel in Nassau. Dealers then received their official invitation to attend a one day national dealer meeting. Upon arrival at this meeting, they found the room appropriately decorated in the theme design.

At regular intervals, during the course of the campaign, a 'league standings' report was sent out to dealerships indicating who held the top position in each league. The actual percentages of sales vs campaign targets were not revealed as this served to provide additional stimulus. A direct mail campaign was also put into operation with dealers receiving overprinted posters of Nassau, photographs of the hotel facilities and recipes for cocktails and local dishes. The campaign proved to be an outstanding success which in itself provided an ideal platform for the launch of the new model range.

Concurrent with the dealer principal programme, the sales team at each dealership were given the opportunity of participating in their own incentive programme and to qualify for various awards. Included in the launch pack given to each member of the sales team at each dealership, was a miniature illustration of a large wall-chart. Colourfully depicting 'outer space' this chart had a number of white spaces dotted all over it, each representing a planet, star, etc. These were numbered, and each had a varying value in terms of prize points. As each sales person made a campaign sale or achieved any stated objective, he or she was invited to sign one space – any vacant space on the chart, freely chosen.

When each space on the chart was completed with a signature, the dealer sales manager or principal called the sales team together for 'the big announcement'.

With due drama the safe was unlocked and a sealed envelope withdrawn. Opening this, the sales manager removed the secret 'space conquest

key card', and read out the number of 'award merits'.

You will see that this chapter's content is turning away from award structures to the actual promotion of the campaign and to the people taking part. Concentration and assembling all the different facets is essential to ensure that your awards and everything else relating to the campaign actually achieve the desired effect – motivate through incentive.

There are no limits to the themes that can be used to promote and sustain an incentive programme. It is a very important creative responsibility and the campaign theme which gives a form and identity to the whole operation, is a peg on which to hang almost everything else. Perhaps the theme is inspired by the award structure. And perhaps the product inspires highly creative themes. Frequently, the theme of the award campaign follows the concurrent consumer advertising campaign which produces an overall 'togetherness' in the marketing thrust, producing even greater awareness for the participant. Enough, then, on themes. But how to give them and the campaign the maximum impact?

Campaign launches

Your campaign launch can be anything from a single colour, one page interdepartmental memorandum from head office mail to theatre, audio-visual, orchestras – even lasers. However, these are extremes. Somewhere between them lies the ideal starting point for your campaign.

If the participants are your own internal employees, the first and easiest method is an announcement in the canteen, but why not find a local pub with a big enough room, probably free if the 'pies and pints' are supplied by the landlord? This initial meeting is an important one.

What is really important is that you launch your incentive campaign with as much impact as possible. Having 'teased', invited and impressed your people, give them a complete launch pack as they leave, also sending a pack to anyone who did not attend. Always have a launch pack, whether it is an A4 sheet of paper or a complete presentation kit. If practicable, towards the end of the launch, include a question and answer session. Accept every question, no matter how naive it may appear and answer it honestly. If your campaign is aimed at participants who have senior area/product sales managers, always brief them, and any union people expressing interest, before the launch meeting.

But do *not* leave it at that! Do *not* expect the impact of the launch to last for more than a fortnight, let alone the entire six months of the programme. There is nothing so boring as yesterday's news, however exciting it was. Today's news, and more probably today's (or tomorrow's) problems will soon assume priority. The remedy is simple. Make yesterday's news today's news, as frequently and with as much impact as possible: in a word, follow-up. Fast-start bonus schemes, already mentioned, can prove an invaluable help.

One word of warning here. Amid all the euphoria and hyperbole of the punchy, whimsical and provocative copywriting that goes into these highly stimulating messages, do not be tempted to publish complete, detailed league tables, showing everyone's results to date in all their stark reality. On the other hand, dramatically announce the superb accomplishments of the fast starters and include and congratulate all who are in the running for the 'grand final award'.

If your campaign has a powerful theme, continue this theme throughout the design and in the copy. However, words and league tables are only one means of communication, there are many others. The one advantage of using paper and card is that with careful planning and a reasonable deadline, the cost of production materials can be reduced.

Fourteen 'starter' ideas

1 Are you using prize point 'cheques', bonus bonds or store vouchers as the award medium? At your launch meeting, why not tape one of these underneath each participant's seat? Having announced the campaign, tell the audience, 'You are all sitting on a fiver, in fact!' Now wait for the first participant to tip the chair and discover the £5 award voucher. Then watch the subsequent impact on the others!

2 Do you plan to invite your people to a hotel for the campaign launch? Why not send each delegate's partner a bouquet of flowers via one of the mailing services?

3 Do you wish to operate a sales programme for the latest model of car? The resultant problem is what to do with the traded-in, three-year old or older used models. Why not print 'prize points cheque' forms in sheets of three, with perforations between each. The top section is worth perhaps 5,000 points, the second 3,000 and the third 2,000 points. One complete sheet of points goes inside each new car.

A new car sale is made with a used car traded in. The sales person brings you the prize point sheet and you write his name on the top cheque. The sales person retains the 5,000 points and places the remaining two cheques in the traded in car. A second sales person sells the latter and receives the second cheque, and the cheque for 2,000 points is placed inside the traded-in old car.

This method motivates the first sales person to sell the new car without any trade-in as it would have earned him all three cheques.

4 The three-part cheque method of award can also be used with the manufacturer providing the awards on sales of new products on condition that the dealer makes an equal contribution in order to dispose of used models and thereby assisting in the financing for new stock.

5 What is your realistic estimate of the demonstrations-to-sales ratio? How does it compare with the industry average? To improve the ratio or maintain it, offer an award per demonstration, provided a sale is made after, say, five demonstrations. Priorities are rapidly recognised by this method.

What if you wish to award only for demonstrations and not for sales? And how do you know that your demonstration team is actually carrying out 22 demonstrations as claimed last month? Simply ask for the name and address of each prospective customer to be included on the claim's award form, and make random checks.

6 Those of you who run hotels, motels or restaurants may be interested in this idea. Give your clients a form on which they can record their assessments of service, amenities, food, etc. Establish an award factor relating to the ratings given by clients with points being awarded. Points can then be divided among those personnel who can positively affect guests' opinion.

7 Do you operate an incentive programme using a merchandise-based prize catalogue? Create campaign knowledge quizzes, with questions to test participants' knowledge of how and why the campaign is being run.

8 Have you ever exposed your people to an award catalogue? If not, then include in your campaign launch pack a 'want list' for each participant and partner and ask them to reply to the following question. 'Imagine you had 15,000 award points to spend, which item(s) would you choose?' And if you add that all 'want lists' will be put into a draw, the volume of the replies may amaze you.

9 Every participant in every programme works for someone or something – home, partner, parents, children. Why not set up a children's painting competition, with age groups, parental endorsements, etc. Try to get the local art school to judge the entries. And award as many good prizes as possible.

10 If your company is unable to stage a launch conference – not even a meeting – a solution could be to produce a reasonably inexpensive recording – by the most senior person in the company – and mail these cassettes to every participant.

11 Are you including a group travel award at the end of your campaign? Why not send everyone a 'map' and ask them to plot the exact route to the destination. The map is marked out, not in miles, but in units of performance or percentage of target needed to be able to qualify. Most recipients will fill in the squares, and 'keeping' the score is a motivational exercise in itself as it continues to focus attention on the incentive activity.

12 Would your participants respond to a challenge? Invite them to set their own target base lines. Each participant at the outset of the programme can either:

(a) accept a 40-unit base line and earn 100 points per unit thereafter;
(b) accept an 80-unit base line and earn 300 points per unit thereafter;
(c) agree to a 100-unit base line and earn 600 points per unit thereafter.

Obviously in this example mathematics have to be accurate, but the concept itself produces a very exciting element.

13 Are you selling direct to the consumer via retail outlets? Here is an idea which is categorised under the heading of 'mystery shopper'. Thoroughly briefed, suitably qualified people to visit your retail outlets at specified times during the campaign period. Whilst maintaining their anonymity, they inspect various aspects of the

retailer's premises and then discreetly complete an assessment form. They then identify themselves to the retailer or dealer and review their findings. Any award that is due is handed to the retailer at that time. This first assessment becomes a base line for future inspections with further points being awarded for improvements over this base figure.

14 Are you planning a superb group travel event for your top dealers? Prior to departure arrange with an overnight 'E6' slide processing establishment to develop slides taken every day. Through out the event, from the welcome party to the banquet on the night before participants return home, numerous 35mm colour slide shots are taken.

Early on the final morning the last slides are mounted and inserted into a sequence. On the last 'get together' prior to returning home the delegates are invited into a conference room. There the participants are shown all the slides taken throughout the event. They see themselves dining, drinking, dancing, laughing, right up to the previous night.

On a more pragmatic note, when flying a party of, say, 50 on a 150-seater flight, why not give your people official welcome cards, valid on both outward and homeward flights for drinks, wine with meals, in-flight headphones, etc. Arrange this when booking the seats.

It is hoped that these ideas will stimulate and prove useful for implementation in your organisation. Perhaps one or more of them may give you an idea of your own on how to attain your specific objectives.

7 The award menu: recognition awards, cash, cash substitutes

Before embarking on the very important review of the various types of awards which can be included in an incentive programme, it is as well to list them and to evaluate their effectiveness. There are four fundamental positive awards, each divisible into several variations.

1 Cash and cash substitutes, such as bonds, certificates, store vouchers, and the like.
2 Recognition symbols such as the cup, shield, trophy, sword of honour and all manner of 'Guild'-type regalia.
3 Merchandise, such as mail order via award points, merits, etc.
4 Travel including group incentive movements, days out, events and family holidays 'bought' with prize points and other award 'currencies'.

Which one of these is likely to be most effective for you? Any one on its own is not sufficient for total motivation. The art – or science – as applied by the motivator is to study the psychological needs of the participant profile, the performance needs of the sponsoring company and financial needs of the budget. And somehow the motivator has to blend them into the most cost-effective compromise.

Many pages of text could be taken up with comparisons but, for the sake of brevity, comprehension, simplicity and retention the table below shows a rough 'credit rating' for each type of award.

Employee behaviour is conditioned by many influences and one of these is known as 'income adjustment'. People get used to a certain style and standard of living and endeavour to maintain it. Any large shift in income is unsettling, more to some than to others. A reasonable increase in income soon becomes the 'norm', and accordingly lifestyle is adjusted upwards. If the income suddenly reverts to its earlier, lower level, another unsettling adjustment takes place. The resultant de-motivation can lower morale and the desire to perform, even below the pre-campaign level.

An even worse situation can arise, however, particularly if people on commission or on output-based earnings are offered cash incentives in a campaign. For example, people earning a fixed commission each month by selling 100 widgets a week are offered 20 per cent more per widget sold during the campaign period. Suddenly, some will reason that they can maintain their fixed monthly income by selling 16.7 per cent fewer widgets a week, and as a result their pace will slacken.

At the end of the programme it is found that this particular group resented the fact that they will in future have to increase their effort to pre-campaign levels in order to earn the same as they did during the programme. Their argument is that if the sponsor can afford to pay 'x' during the campaign, why could they not continue to be paid this on a regular basis? Whilst cash-based programmes are easy to introduce, they are sometimes very difficult to terminate without the

Table 5. Comparison and evaluation of various types of awards

Desiderata	Cash, etc.	Recognition awards	Merchandise	Travel, etc.
Family influence: will the whole family be excited by the incentive offered?	No: the family consider cash just a small addition to regular income – if they ever get to hear about it.	No: usually the family hears about this award only after it is won and then only by the winner's family.	Yes: most families select awards and encourage participants to earn them. (See Note 1)	Maybe: only if the participant and his family feel they have a good chance to qualify for an award.
Choice: will all participants be able to select the award they want most?	Yes: although cash will often disappear in routine household bills.	No: self-explanatory.	Yes. (See Note 2)	Group travel – No. Family holiday award – Yes.
Number of winners: can all participants win according to performance?	Yes: the amount can be in proportion to effort.	No: if they could, it would not be recognised.	Yes: in proportion to effort and results.	Group travel – No. Family holiday award – Yes.
Appeal to average: will the awards appeal greatly to the middle 80% of participants?	Maybe: some may feel they will be inadequately rewarded for goals assigned.	No: self-explanatory.	Yes: even a relatively inexpensive prize award can be a much desired luxury.	Group travel – No. Family holiday award – Perhaps.

Pride: will the award cause winners to enjoy maximum praise and acclaim?	Hardly: except for family, who would show friends a bank deposit entry?	Yes: definitely when the rules are equitable.	Yes: the participant is recognised as being an award winner.	Yes: another form of top recognition award.
Excitement: can the awards be widely and powerfully promoted?	No: there is nothing more ordinary than cash.	Yes: until participants realise who will or will not win.	Yes: participants look forward to earning awards they feel they cannot afford to buy.	Yes: nothing is more powerful.
Lasting value: will the award be a long lasting reminder of success?	No: cash as an award disappears as soon as it is pocketed, deposited or spent.	Yes: obviously.	Yes: also has use and enjoyment values.	Yes: if everything goes well.
Cost: is the cost of the award good value for what you paid for it?	Maybe: but what happens when the campaign and award terminates? (See Note 3)	Yes: and it usually costs so little.	Yes.	Yes: group incentive travel also has features that individuals and money cannot buy.

Note 1 Families are inveterate browsers. If you show them as well as tell them what they can set their sights on, you will make *your* objectives live in their minds through *their* objectives.

Note 2 Analysis of many thousands of merchandise award orders shows that some 75 per cent of items are partner/home orientated, 15 per cent home/children orientated and the participant seldom gains more than 10 per cent.

Note 3 This is important and deserves an illustration of its own. Here is the 'time and motive study' of the typical motivation programme.

Fig 3: Time and Motive Study

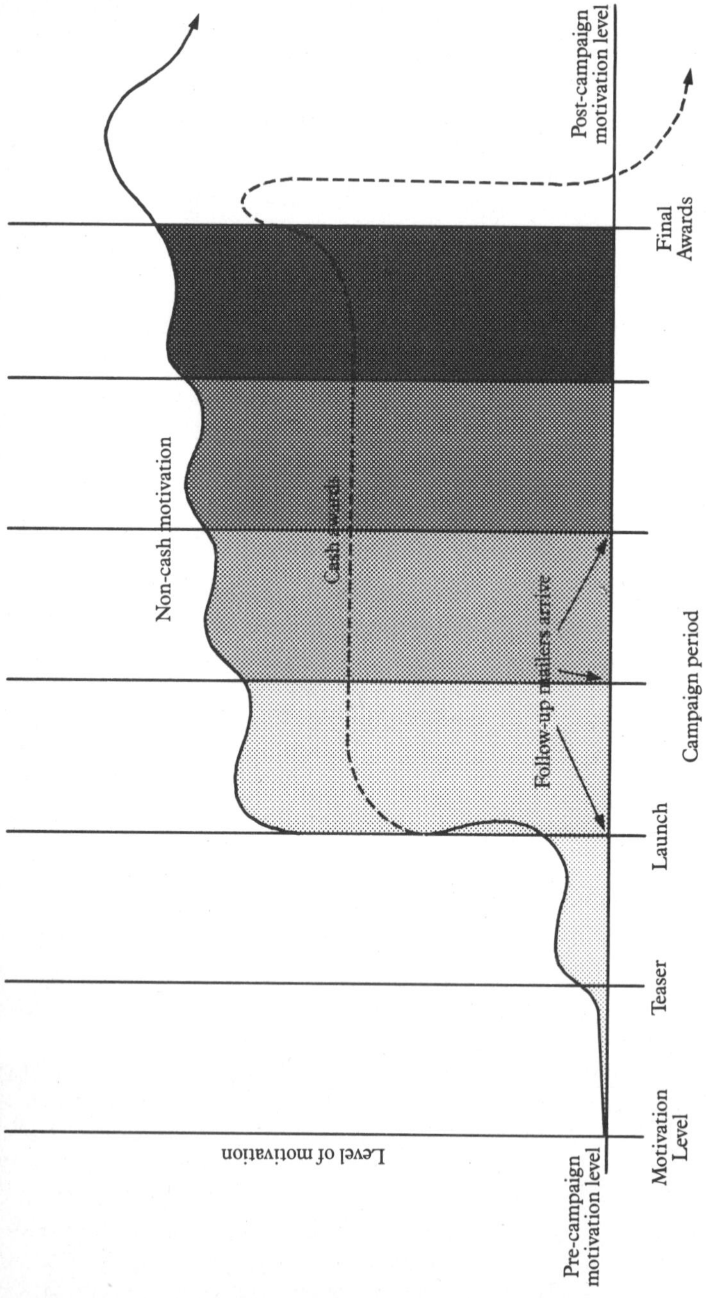

loss of goodwill. And yet cash is used as a form of incentive all the time.

Wages and salaries motivate people to be available for work and to put in enough effort in order to keep the job. Commissions, etc, cause some to maintain a productivity level which will meet the demands of their current level of comfort. Even if you increase the cash, you will not achieve better results from most people. If cash were to be a proven motivator, every sales agent working on a commission-only basis would be a workaholic with a long list of material assets and possessions to his credit.

It is true to say that amongst the largest, more important and continuous users of merchandise and/or travel-based incentive programmes, can be included self-employed participants – from such industries as insurance, double-glazing, home party selling and cosmetics. Virtually all these people are paid on a commission-only basis yet all the sponsors or manufacturers concerned have repeatedly proven that motivation programmes are an absolutely essential ingredient in their marketing plans, particularly in attaining specific tactical objectives throughout the year.

So what is the incentive value of cash substitutes such as bonds, vouchers, coupons and similar media? If the award budget was to be spread over a number of people then the result is considerable. Bonds are cash – and yet not quite. They can provide a proportion of the desire of both needs, i.e. winning and acquiring. Provided the retail or departmental store personnel are aware that the bonds or vouchers represent pride in skill and hard work, and that bond shoppers are special people, choosing and claiming their award in a favourite local precinct or high street shop is a rewarding experience. Admittedly, the bond winners can add cash of their own, which lessens the association the award has with your programme but, on the other hand, the item(s) with which they proudly leave the store would not be theirs without that programme.

In these days of rapid model change, merchandise in stores may be ahead of items in a year-old points catalogue which was compiled perhaps a year before it was actually published. Finally, there is always the truism that, once in the store with their bonds or vouchers to hand, 'if they don't see what they want, they might want what they see'.

During the late 1960s and throughout the 1970s, trading stamps were extensively used as a cash-substitute incentive award media. During that time virtually all filling stations and half the supermarkets in the UK were giving customers either green, pink or gold stamps based on their purchases. The stamp company, in their further efforts to expand their business, then sold their stamps to those organisations who sought to reward their participants with a media which could be added to those being collected at the petrol stations and the grocery stores, thereby reducing the 'saving time' for the delivery of a desired item of merchandise.

The least expensive incentive award of all is the cup, trophy or gold-plated medal. And the effect on those two or three recognition-hungry star performers who are invited to the stage at the annual conference to receive such symbols of praise can be dramatic. But never make the mistake of using recognition awards or symbols alone. After all it would be self-defeating to award 450 swords of honour among a participant listing of 500. The value of a recognition award is its scarcity! It has been said that the silver plaque – or the top recognition award – is the cherry on the icing on the incentive cake.

8 The award menu: merchandise, and speciality days or weekends

Merchandise

From the evaluations given to merchandise in Chapter 6, you will appreciate its value as a tangible award. However, you are not in the fringe benefit business. Profit is your objective: profit from people power. You will have observed that the value of merchandise is that it motivates more people to a greater degree than anything so far in this book. If you can, with 80 sales people, motivate 240 home-based 'family supporters' to work for your interests in the success of your campaign, then success is almost inevitable.

By introducing your merchandise awards into each participant's home, you succeed (assuming each has one partner and one child) in having 240 people enthusiastically supporting your objectives. The most efficient way is by the use of the catalogue, or the award collection, of course! Anything from one dozen to two thousand items of use and beauty: personal and family luxuries in glossy, four-colour detail and each 'priced' in the appropriate award currency.

Inserted into a gusset within the back cover is the award index: detailing each item and the number of points or merits or award media required to obtain it. Also at the back are forms. These should be completed by the participants when they have accumulated sufficient to 'afford' the selected item. Originally the majority of the points came in the form of documents, 'cheques' or certificates, which were collected, stored and closely guarded. They were then attached to a completed award order form and mailed to the company for redemption. In most instances the procedure is now computerised.

The participant is registered in the sponsoring company's award 'bank', with a personal numbered account. Each award of points and each award order is automatically credited or debited to that account and recorded on regularly despatched award 'statements'. These frequently incorporate a bulletin merchandise order form for future redemptions.

However, apart from featuring the awards, the catalogue provides a constant reminder of personal objectives, particularly if the campaign follow-up provokes re-scanning of its pages. Its cover provides an ideal opportunity to dramatise the campaign theme, together with a personal message from the most senior executive in the company (complete with photograph), the announcement, rules, the award schedules and the details of the entire campaign.

The arrival of the catalogue is the signal for the whole family to join in the target-setting, or sights-setting as it is actually called. If a young member yearns for a bicycle and the family agree that it is one of the awards that are within their reach, the participant is going to make every effort to win as the only way of getting it is by achieving the required results.

At the end of the programme, or at any stage when sufficient points have been earned, the much desired bicycle can be obtained merely by

sending off the order. Shortly afterwards it will be delivered and presented with due ceremony. The participant – the award winner – becomes a hero in his own home, not just merely a breadwinner.

Whilst confirming that proper utilisation of an attractive catalogue or collection of merchandise awards can be one of the most effective motivation vehicles that exists, the catalogue production teams do, on occasions, encounter difficult problems. One of these problems is the long 'lead time' that exists from the time the merchandise is selected through to the ultimate ordering by and delivery to the participant. This can, on occasions, span two years.

As a result, it is inevitable that 'non-availability' situations occur. Difficulties can also develop in times of fast rising inflation when it becomes necessary to increase the number of points or merits required for the merchandise items as catalogue suppliers are forced to increase their prices. Ask any catalogue-based incentive company what their publication department will be doing on the day after the current year's catalogue is sent to the printer. The answer will be 'starting on next year's, of course'. So, with research, negotiation, selection, pricing, etc. of up to 1,500 or more items from up to 750 different suppliers, your participants could be ordering an item that went out of production nine months ago. The better the resources of the incentive company, the more their buying power and the greater your protection against such problems.

To assist in dealing with the requirements of the Inland Revenue (see Chapter 10 for details) many incentive companies offer their clients and participants a proportionate pricing plan. The prize point 'price' or requirement for the items in the catalogue represent sometimes 80 per cent of the overall cost to the sponsoring company who then pays the incentive company the required

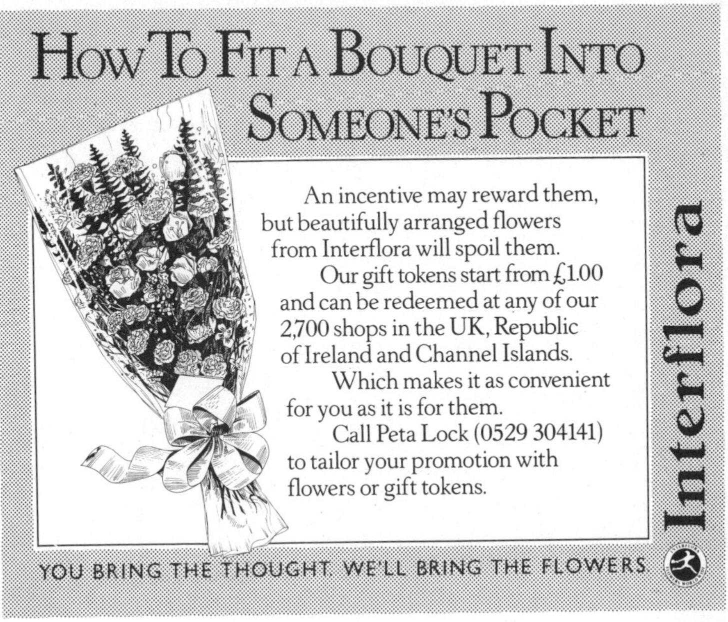

balance percentage (20 per cent in this example) as a service charge on all the points redeemed in the vast majority of cases. The participant is then assessed for income tax on the 80 per cent and not on the full 100 per cent.

It goes without saying that a properly researched merchandise award catalogue represents the crystallisation of many years of experience in two disciplines: purchase negotiations and motivational psychology. Both skills are essential as without either success will not come.

The incentive catalogue content must contain a wide enough 'price' range to suit all campaign budgets and award-winning opportunities, from a package of monogrammed hand-embroidered handkerchiefs to – as was once featured – a light aircraft!

The number of awards available at each rising

price bracket must be such that choice is reasonably high at lower value, and increases on a carefully plotted curve up to total content. There must be only a few limited items in the high price bracket so as to avoid doubts on the realism of the incentive programme. All these imponderables are further complicated by the need to appeal to every conceivable need and desire.

The merchandise catalogue fully deserves a special place since it is totally and fundamentally different from most mail-order books. There may be lower priced items in the glossy pages but there are no 'bargain basement' goods whatsoever. Famous brand names are a 'must', with the vast majority of them pitched at an aspirational level in the minds of participants.

The catalogue remains in the home for up to a year and every item has to be 'top quality' as well as the incentive company providing a good service. If either the merchandise or the handling of it disappoints in any way, it is the sponsoring company who is held to blame in the eyes of the participant. As the incentive company is well aware of this, they should make doubly sure that the awards are such that each participant is proud to possess them.

An "experience"

And now to introduce a relative newcomer which is rapidly gaining popularity in the selection of incentive awards: an experience. This is something that should appeal to a part of the participant's character. It could be nothing more exotic than a meal and a show and staying the night away at a first class hotel. Possibly the idea of a totally different atmosphere would help. An Elizabethan banquet with 'strolling players' maybe?

Another completely new industry has developed, and it is moving into is own particular niche for award consideration. If your participants include a number of sensation-hungry types, you can now

offer them a dazzling selection of satisfactions or experiences, of which the 'night on the town' is only one. Are they golfers? There is a plethora of days and weekends to choose from, including coaching from the top professional, and a round at one of the world's most famous courses. And why not let them play with golf clubs earned from the merchandise catalogue!

Does your company employ active types? Send them on a battle course, with real weapons firing soluble paint and a sniper behind every third tree. Granted, a bit bizarre. What about having a treasure hunt? Slightly more sedentary, but appealing to every 'who-dunnit' fan, is a weekend in manor houses or country hotels on a gruesome but intriguing trail of a murderer.

Have you any budding stuntmen and racing drivers? Let them loose on specialist land and water buggies and hovercraft under supervision.

There really is an award to satisfy everyone. The fulfilment of psychological needs is represented by more than cash, recognition symbols, merchandise and travel. And informed companies have realised that their marketing success depends on meeting people's needs. So there is no need to restrict your thinking, your imagination, your creativity in the field of actual awards.

The experiences related above are, as mentioned, relative newcomers to the award media for motivation programmes. However, 'old timers' in this category are a day at the races at Ascot, the Derby, or a day at Henley or Wimbledon: all complete with smoked salmon, strawberries and cream, and champagne.

9 The award menu: incentive travel – the icing on the cake

What is incentive travel? Here are a few things it is not: It is not the result of a sudden whim to provide a 'jolly' for the boys and girls. Nor is it an opportunity for the director or sales manager to visit somewhere he had always wanted to. It is certainly not a package tour or 'off-the-shelf' holiday, with a cocktail party bolted on at the beginning and a farewell banquet welded on at the end. Nor is it an exercise in shopping around for the biggest discounts on offer – or a supposedly real bargain buy – or trying to cut costs at every available corner and on every conceivable occasion.

Incentive travel is not a new concept, in fact the first professionally organised incentive travel campaign in the UK was operated some 25 years ago by E F MacDonald. The demands and requirements of that particular programme all those years ago are exactly the same as they are today. Nothing much has changed as far as that is concerned. Incentive travel has been a major marketing weapon in the US for over 40 years. Travel is in fact the top group award in a carefully structured motivation programme, designed to reward those participants who achieve the objectives established at the outset by the sponsoring company. It is, or most certainly should be, a prestigious award which has been worked for. But incentive travel is often just one of the ingredients in the total incentive award mix. There almost certainly should be many other types of awards featured and promoted in the overall motivation plan, to ensure the achievement of the sponsor's objectives. Incentive travel does represent the ultimate recognition in a well-balanced programme. However, a word of caution. Due to its relatively high cost, incentive travel is nearly always structured on some form of competitive basis. There are invariably more losers than winners, and this is a very important point to bear in mind when developing a motivational campaign. It confirms the important psychological requirement to try whenever and wherever possible to establish a comprehensive selection of awards in order to encourage maximum stimulation throughout the sponsoring company's organisation. In the eyes of all participants, there should be no losers, only winners.

The company should carefully construct its motivational programme. It should carry out all the necessary research to identify its needs, clearly defining its business goals and the time period to achieve these. It should accurately determine those who can assist in achieving these goals and, finally, the company should calculate the budget available on achievement.

Assume that after properly apportioning selections of the overall budget to other award media (merchandise, bonds, prize holidays, etcetera) to launch meetings, promotional material, etcetera, a sum of, say, £50,000 is available for incentive travel for the top producer in the programme. After establishing how many (including partners) should qualify, the next area to look is the selection of suitable destinations, balancing these against the travel costs, the time taken to get there, and so on. It should go without saying that the incentive travel programme must be promoted and operated throughout your company on a 'VIP Plus' basis.

The ultimate award winners must be regarded – and seen to be regarded – as personal guests of the management and treated accordingly. Ideally, the programme should be designed so that there is no need for any award winner to pay out a single penny except for personal souvenirs.

No matter how superb your programme, or how magnificent the destination and ground content, it is essential that your travel award be promoted throughout the entire campaign period. It is the belief of most experts in the field of incentive travel that: 'if all sales persons were single there would be no motivational industry to speak of. The power of the spouse and family is never to be underestimated when it comes to encouraging corporate employees to exceed a sales quota or participate in a meeting away from home' (Harry Redman, *Corporate and Incentive Travel*, February, 1987).

Effective promotion is also necessary in conveying the attractiveness and allure that your chosen destination has to offer. Overall promotional strategy, destination-related literature and gifts all bring the incentive campaign into the home at very little expense.

When planning the entertainment, do not expect hotel staff to provide all the uniqueness, creative thinking or implementation necessary to make the campaign a success. It is not their responsibility. Imagination can make all the difference in the world between a good incentive trip and a mediocre one. As an example, select any hotel ballroom, add a handful of musicians, who are usually versatile and cooperative, a chef who is willing to be creative, a few costumes from a local theatrical rental shop or community theatre and some props and decorations. You can

transform that ballroom from a baronial hall into a medieval one, a civic hall ballroom into the café that Bogart owned in Casablanca. These are just a few ideas. There are countless others.

Further ideas of the ingenuity behind the unforgettable can be gained from a few 'thumbnail sketches'. On the departure day it is usual practice for the incentive travel company to install a hospitality desk or counter at the appropriate airport concourse. Some companies will invite, at their expense, the award winners to stay overnight at the airport hotel prior to a morning departure, and perhaps stage a 'welcome' cocktail party or 'get together' dinner, all of which would have been considered in the initial budget planning. On board the aircraft, whether it is scheduled or chartered, award winners would receive 'open bar treatment'. Upon arrival at the destination, a special welcome greeting could be arranged for the award winners.

When organising the campaign, check with the airline's ground handling agent to see if any assistance can be provided to enable a speedy clearance through immigration and customs. This again affords additional recognition of the group.

During the transfer from the airport to hotel, room keys together with other hotel information should be issued. It is sometimes a good idea to budget for a 'greetings cocktail' party immediately the group arrives at the hotel whilst the baggage is being delivered to the rooms.

It is usually standard operating procedure for award winners to find a gift awaiting them upon arrival in their rooms, and it is also quite normal for sponsors to distribute room gifts every night throughout the programme. The president of one sponsoring company includes among the room gifts a silver charm for award winners' wives; the charm itself relates to the destination. First-time winners receive a silver charm bracelet so each time the dealer qualifies for an award trip his wife receives another silver charm to add to her bracelet.

Each day's programme should be action-packed with a variety of facilities on offer. Another suggestion, where and when possible, is to plan for meals to be taken at different locations every day. If you have a large group, for example, and it is difficult to accommodate all of them for a meal outside the hotel properly, break them up into smaller groups and utilise smaller and more intimate restaurants on a 'mystery dine-around' basis.

Special attention should be given to organising emergency 'bad weather' activities especially when using seaside or resort area destinations. During initial planning, see if the hotel has an in-house film and/or large screen video facility. And if so then ensure that two or three films (in the relevant languages) accompany the group. Nothing can be more intimidating than having 250 people sitting around the lobby of a hotel with the rain pouring down outside – no golf, no tennis, no swimming, no sightseeing – with all eyes fixed on the tour director!

Before concluding this chapter on incentive travel, a word about those who do not qualify for the Bali, Bermuda or Barbados extravaganza. These participants can still earn and qualify for incentive travel. Most incentive companies have a type of 'currency' award which can be exchanged in full – or part – for selected 'package' holidays. While the star performers are on safari en route between Nairobi and Mombassa, other participants who have done well but not quite as well, can choose where to go, for how long and whom to take. It may be the Mediterranean, or even closer to home, but it is still a holiday that they have been able to earn and one which they might not have experienced without the campaign.

A word of caution here as sometimes luck can play its part in the operation of a travel award movement. Good luck, hopefully, as experienced in Monte Carlo by a group of automotive dealer parts managers.

The managers' itinerary for the last evening included dinner at *La Salle des Etoiles* and later being taken to the famous casino in Monte Carlo. Each parts manager was awarded £20 worth of chips, together with an invitation to 'break the proverbial bank'. But when the tour director met the Maitre d'Hotel at *La Salle* to check out the room layout, dinner menu and other arrangements for the evening, on learning that the group would be leaving the restaurant immediately after the meal a shocked Maitre d'Hotel gasped, 'Pourquoi Monsieur, do you not know what is happening here tonight?'

Included in this huge building accommodating *La Salle des Etoiles* was a new casino, to be opened that evening by Prince Rainier. The opening was to be followed by a spectacular international cabaret show, which the group would miss by returning to the old casino. Furthermore, all this glamour, with the Rainiers in attendance at a nearby table, was included in the price of the dinner. A quick change of plan was called for. And the result was an evening never to be forgotten with the chips issued for the old casino being made valid for the new one.

Whilst tactical incentive travel programmes can be utilised for the short term, say for the three-month achievement of specific objectives, many companies are now introducing continuous, year-long programmes in which every possible aspect of dealership effectiveness is addressed and recognised. The eventual award comprises of an invitation from the president or the chairman of the company to attend a very prestigious function. The programme may include a full evening dress banquet or gala ball, indeed sometimes a complete castle and grounds are taken over by the party. Overall, a very special occasion and event.

Whilst dealing with the subject of incentive travel, it must be mentioned that 'cruising' is becoming increasingly popular. Life on the ocean waves, however short, certainly offers different attractions. Top-name entertainers are present on many cruises. All this is combined with the opportunity of visits to exotic and interesting places, the ambience of the ship, and the food and entertainment.

Many companies hold the view that there are few better incentives than cruises. Modern vessels with stabilisers reduce the likelihood of passengers suffering from seasickness.

Chartering an entire vessel is a developing trend. The advantages are that there is no competition from other passengers and, within the operating standards of the ship, itineraries can be made to measure. To charter a ship on the basis of total occupancy (depending on the vessel's tonnage, of course) can be economical, but this, of course, depends on your budget.

One final point, when determining the number of company personnel in an award-winning group, consideration should be given on whether or not to include the company doctor on your overseas programme, particularly if the selected destination has a reputation for unsettled stomachs or other medical disorders. Health standards in many countries are not as good as our own, and should your group suffer a bout of sickness, it may well work out to be cheaper to be prepared. Couple this to the fact that the very presence of a known practitioner provides a great deal of confidence and generally adds to the comfort level of the programme.

10 Tax implications for the company

The taxation levies on various forms of motivation awards vary considerably from country to country. Some overseas governments make little or no provision when dealing with motivation awards and have yet to acknowledge that the position needs to be clarified. Indeed, in the UK conditions differ between one part of the country and another because the interpretation of what qualifies for tax levies or exemptions can be assessed differently between individual tax inspectors.

As a result of the uncertainties and the 'mystique' surrounding areas of taxation there can be little doubt that many companies have elected not to run these risks. And this has certainly been to the detriment of those segments of commerce and industry which would otherwise, had the position been clear, become involved in setting up motivational award programmes.

An untold number of companies have created incentive programmes without sufficient research into the tax implications of their awards. To this day many live with the possibilities that they, their employees together with wholesalers, retailers and others could receive notification from the Inland Revenue investigating past programmes, with the resultant demand for payment to be made.

It would not be practicable for these pages to attempt a resumé of even a selection of the laws of taxation in different countries, and it would serve little purpose anyway. Therefore, this book concentrates on the tax implications in the UK.

It is an inescapable fact that virtually all 'benefits in kind', regardless of their nature, are subject to taxation. This, of course, includes all awards earned during the period of an incentive programme.

Incentives are receiving a more structured approach from the Inland Revenue these days. The days of horse-traded composite rates with the friendly local inspector are over. If an employee (or any third party for that matter) receives a benefit in the course of his or her job, it is taxed at the standard rate of income tax, ranging from the standard rate up to the top band of tax.

Included in these considerations of 'benefits in kind' are:

1 Incentive awards of goods, services, travel.
2 Vouchers exchangeable for goods, services, etc.
3 Campaign celebrations.
4 Conferences to the degree that they are personal benefit and not a clearly proveable business activity.
5 High value recognition items.

The Inland Revenue's interpretation is becoming clearer with the settling in of the Incentive Valuation Unit formed in late 1984. This unit can be very helpful. They listen to incentive sponsors' viewpoints and their decisions are reasonable *but arguable*. Here is an example for your own guidance, relating to foreign study tours and business conferences, which illustrates the Inland Revenue's approach.

A director may contend that his overseas tour or conference is in no sense a holiday and that it must therefore have been a necessary business trip. He will stress the mileage covered, the number and nature of the places visited, the consequent fatigue and the lack of time for demonstrably recreational activities. All this, however, is beside the point, since in these matters it does not automatically follow that because an expense was not incurred in taking a holiday it must of necessity have been incurred in doing one's job ... Similarly, you do not prove that an expense was necessarily incurred for one purpose by showing that it was not incurred for some other purpose. The critical tests are those imposed by Section 189(1) ICTA 1970 and the tax consequences will depend largely on the facts of the case. This shows the need to record the business activities of a conference if a successful case for relief from tax is to be upheld. So, how can 'incentives' continue to motivate when some time later (often years) a tax bill comes tumbling in?

Sponsors of incentives can pay tax at the standard rate on behalf of the participants provided they enter into a formal contract with the Inland Revenue under their provisions for taxed award incentive schemes. This provision would allow tax-paid incentives to be awarded to participants provided their personal taxable income does not exceed £17,900 (1986/87). So to summarise, this would apply to:

1 A married man with gross income of £21,695.
2 A single person with gross income of £20,325. This probably covers the majority of incentive participants. But if you are applying for a formal contract, give them all the facts.
3 In addition to the requirements of their own fact sheets (p443, p440, p35 (TAS) (1986)) you should provide:

(a) detailed budgets;

(b) details of the award media.

The sponsor will get taxed on values of the:

1 Reward.
2 Celebrations.
3 High value recognition items.

The sponsor will *not* get taxed on costs of:

1 Launching the programme.
2 Administration.
3 Communication pieces.
4 Handling and distributing the above administrative aspects.
5 Printing.
6 Agency and management fee.
7 Data processing.

Higher rates of tax *cannot* be paid by the sponsors of incentive programmes. The ultimate rates to be applied are specific to the individual in any fiscal year and only determinable when all 'returns' are received. Nor would it be possible to calculate the appropriate personal tax cost of an incentive programme to enable the supplier to offer it 'tax paid'.

Basic 'emoluments' are increased or reduced by the incidence of:

1 'Benefits in kind' – cars, private health insurance, company payment of private costs – P11D items.
2 Wives with high earning where income is aggregated.
3 Business Expansion Scheme investment allowance.
4 Loss-making business activities.

The problem is obvious for higher-rate taxpayers and the de-motivation is there. If a 60 per cent taxpayer receives £2,000 in a taxed award scheme where the standard rate of tax of 29 per cent has already been paid, he faces a bill of £873.24 for the difference.

	£
Basic value of 'award'	2,000.00
Tax at 29 per cent of gross up value	816.90
Grossed-up value of total paid supplier	2,816.90
Tax at 60 per cent of grossed-up value	1,690.14
Standard rate paid by provider	816.90
Amount payable by beneficiary	873.24

It is a fact of life for many senior executives (usually franchised dealers whose supplying manufacturers are engaged in major motivation programmes) that their direct involvement in programmes and events is unavoidable by virtue of their importance within the 'organisation'.

The New System as applied to companies

On 1 November 1984, the Inland Revenue announced the start of a 'new system' in the taxing of incentive awards. After this date, any company that wishes to start non-cash award campaigns but who wishes to account for the basic rate tax liability themselves, must adopt this system. Previous arrangements made with the Revenue no longer apply.

If this system affects your campaign you are required to contact the specifically established office of the Inland Revenue *before* you start planning. (The address is 4th Floor, 27 Broadwick Street, London W1.) They will in turn ask you to supply them with all the details of the proposed campaign, plus details of the participants so that all this information can be set down in a formal contract between the Revenue and your company. A point to note here: if you are paying the tax on behalf of your participants then you are required to include *all* of them – selection, in this instance, is not possible.

Basic rate tax is applied to the grossing-up of the gross taxable value of the awards. The tax is then due within 90 days from the end of the tax year in which the awards were made. When making this payment you will need to submit to your local Inland Revenue office a 35-type document. This contract must show (for awards with a total gross value of £100):

(a) the name of the recipient;
(b) the name of the recipient's employer;
(c) the address of the recipient's place of work;
(d) the taxation status of each individual;
(e) the gross taxable value of the awards provided; and
(f) the tax attributable to the gross taxable value of the awards.

At the end of this list (value sub-totalled) you must list an aggregate of all awards, and the tax payable, made to employees whose total gross taxable awards in that year were £100 or less.

In turn, it is your responsibility to provide your employees with a certificate showing the following information. (All these forms can be obtained from the Revenue.)

(a) the incentive scheme's tax reference number;
(b) the company's name;
(c) the employee's name;
(d) the address where the employee works;
(e) the income tax year in which the award was made;
(f) the gross taxable value of the award;
(g) the tax payable on that award.

You will also have to state, in writing, that your company will be accountable to the Inland Revenue for the tax due. Do discuss this matter carefully with your company accountant as tax planning may be possible.

The Revenue require – and supply – that a

contract must be entered into for such arrangements. However, it can be terminated giving 90 days' notice.

If you are offering an incentive to a self-employed person or a company (say a distributor) then for purposes of these arrangements the grossing-up and reporting procedures outlined on the previous pages will not apply. Instead, you can make the award without deducting basic rate tax, but you must notify the Inspector of Taxes, telling him the name and address of the participant and the cost of the award. You should again provide a certificate showing the details that have been supplied to the inspector.

For employees earning under £8,500 per annum, including the value of the incentives earned, the Revenue are prepared to take the second-hand value of the goods provided in an incentive programme. However, you will need to supply proof of the level of the reward payable to your lower level earners and details of what they have been offered as an incentive ('reward'). The Revenue's criteria appears to be what values the goods would fetch if sold for cash!

What does the future hold?

Higher taxpayers will be disappointed when reading these pages and ask, naturally, 'can anything be done for them?', as the motivating factor appears to have been taken out of any incentive campaign by the Revenue. The Chancellor appears to be sympathetic to the concept of incentives in business – no doubt mindful that higher sales equals higher profit and more revenue for his coffers. A Green Paper entitled *Profit Related Pay* proposes that remuneration related to business profit performance is worthy of special tax treatment. But it is not known whether this will be passed on to the statute books and so aid your higher paid employees.

In essence, the new system involves all cases of non-cash awards and makes no distinction between the source of supply. Whatever campaign you are planning, do ensure that your taxable situation is covered.

11 Where do you go from here?

The previous pages will, it is hoped, have provided you with some insights into the theories and practices of motivation. It is further hoped that the suggestions and ideas provided will encourage you either to consider introducing incentive programmes into your company or perhaps into your own area of responsibility for the first time. On the other hand, it may furnish you with additional input.

'*Motivating through Incentives*' will cease to develop and evolve only when profit is no longer of importance or when there is no one remaining to motivate. Motivation, as a commercially exploitable discipline, may have been accidentally stumbled upon in 1922 but what started as a tool has since become a technology. This technology has discovered the science that supports it and has developed into a multi-million pound, multinational industry involving thousands of employees in different disciplines all grouped together.

It is certain that the need to motivate people will become an increasingly important factor which will have to be recognised and addressed

by an increasing number of industries and commercial organisations.

As the comfort levels of people continue to rise – dictated by ever improving living standards – so it will create further difficulties to extract more than an average performance from your employees. Salary or wage increments will almost certainly not produce comparable increased productivity, let alone the extra profit required to meet these additional expenses. In fact, it could be argued that if large salary increases are given and other benefits in kind are increased or added to the compensation package this could result in a general lessening of productivity.

Since World War II, we have seen the steady reduction in working man-hours from a 48 hour week to 44 hour week down to its present level. Further reduction in working hours will have an impact on overall productivity. Your job as motivator will grow in importance as companies realise that whatever time is utilised has got to be used to its maximum productivity. Thus the need for *'Motivating through Incentives'* – indeed one could almost say 'motivation for existence' – will reach an even higher level of importance than its level today.

Everyone involved in the business of the creation and development of motivation programmes must understand and realise that by far the most important requirement is 'creativity'. For example, national tourist authorities must exert themselves towards discovering and promoting local facilities which in turn will make their various locations somewhere exciting to visit. They must create stimulating packages which will result in the final incentive travel decision-maker saying: 'Right, we'll take our incentive group there next year – they've got something new, exciting and different to offer.'

On reading through this book and having decided to instigate some form of incentive activity within your company, you might assume

CAVENDISH COLLECTION

Whatever your requirements for company ties and scarves CAVENDISH COLLECTION can provide the ideal solution.

Excellent free design service, top quality Printed and Woven silks and polyesters all backed by a high professional service.

If you want the the best contact the best.

CAVENDISH COLLECTION

For further information contact:

Janice Chambers
Cavendish Collection
Bourne Road, Crayford, Kent DA1 4BP
Tel. No. 0322 522129

HOW TO EXPAND YOUR CLIENT'S BUSINESS BY TAKING HIS MIND OFF WORK...

If you want proof that the Guinness Book of Records will make a riveting promotional tool, just put it in reception. We guarantee your client's will pick it up and not want to put it down.

It's the world's most popular book, it's compulsive reading, it's full of success stories. And one of those success stories could be yours.

We can also offer over 70 other titles ranging from rock music to reference allowing endless opportunities to custom make books for your company or clients.

If you would like further information please ring Chris Groves on **01–367 4567.**

it is absolutely essential to call in one of the incentive companies to assist in the creation and development of a campaign. This, of course, is not a must. From further study of the pages within this book, you will be able to construct a very workable, worthwhile and profitable plan for your organisation and, at the same time, avoid some of the pitfalls that may otherwise have caused you problems.

While it is foreseen that the need for the motivation of personnel will not change in the coming years (in fact the only change will be the need to address it with even greater determination and expertise), there is, of course, the possibility of a change in emphasis in the stimulus provided by the rewards themselves. Awards over the years have shown their motivational pulling power by the success levels achieved and their subsequent continued usage. But as time goes by new

elements will no doubt be introduced into the awards media and these, in turn, will have to prove themselves to be at least equal to or more effective than those utilised by the industry today. The need for constant updates and product information is therefore vital, if you are to stay in touch.

In conclusion, creativity at all stages and levels within industry and commerce is of paramount importance. It is the key if you and your company are to continue to benefit from '*Motivating through Incentives*'.

Appendix I

Media listing

Conference Britain
2 Queensway
Redhill, Surrey RH1 1QS

Conferences & Exhibitions International
2 Queensway
Redhill, Surrey RH1 1QS

Conference World
(Association of Conference Executives International)
Conference Publications Ltd
Woodlands House
Hall Hill, Brigstock
Kettering, Surrey

Incentive Today
Langfords Publications Ltd
32 West Street
Brighton BR1 2RT

Incentive Travel World
Maclaren Publishers Ltd
PO Box 109
Maclaren House
19 Scarbrook Road
Croydon CR9 1QH

Marketing
Haymarket Magazines Ltd
22 Lancaster Gate
London W2 3LY

Marketing Week
60 Kingly Street
London W1R 5LH

Meetings & Incentive Travel (incorporating Venue)
Herontye House
Stuart Way
East Grinstead
Sussex RH19 4QA

Promotions & Incentives
Maclaren Publishers Ltd
PO Box 109
Maclaren House
19 Scarbrook Road
Croydon CR9 1QH

What's new in Marketing
Morgan-Grampian House
Calderwood Street
Woolwich
London SE18 6QH

Appendix II

Where to go for help and advice

A number of incentive companies, travel operators and other suppliers have formed themselves into associations in order to exchange ideas and experiences and to market and promote the facilities and services they represent. Each of the associations featured below have motivational and incentive specialists within their respective memberships.

ACE International	Association of Conference Executives Riverside House High Street, Huntingdon Cambridgeshire PE18 6SG
AIR	Arbeitsgemeinschaft Incentivereisen Sternstrasse 63a D-4000 Dusseldorf 30 German Federal Republic
AFPTA	Association Française de Professionel du Tourisme d'Affaires 9 Boulevard Maleshercles F-75009 Paris France

EUROMIC	European Meetings and Incentives Consortium 67 Rue de Richelieu F-75002 Paris France
ICCA	International Congress and Convention Association JW Brouwersplein 27 PO Box 5343 1007 AH Amsterdam Netherlands
ITA:UK	Incentive Travel Association of the United Kingdom 52 Saint Maries Grove Richmond Surrey
ITMAN	Incentive Travel Management Association Netherlands Sonesta Hotel Kattegt 1 NL-1012 SZ Amsterdam Netherlands
IDMA	International Destination Management Association Maurkirchnerstr. 4 D-8000 München 80 German Federal Republic

Appendix III

Incentive shows and exhibitions

International Confex, London
January
Business Design Centre
PEL Communications
PO Box 33W, Heron House
Wembley, Middlesex HA9 9NU

Incentive Marketing Exhibition, Brighton
April
MacLaren Exhibitions Ltd
PO Box 138
Token House, 79–81 High Street
Croydon CR9 3SS

Meetings & Incentive Travel Exposition, New York
May
Jacob Javits Convention Center
Thalheim Expositions Inc.
42 Bayview Avenue, PO Box 4200
Manhasset NY, USA

The European Incentive & Business Travel & Meetings Exhibition – Palexpo Centre, Geneva
May
EIBTM, Langfords International Exhibitions plc
32 West Street
Brighton, Sussex BN1 2RT

The National Incentive & Promotion
Exhibition, London
June
Langfords Exhibitions Ltd
32 West Street
Brighton, Sussex BN1 2RT

Meetings Market Place, London
June
Association of Conference Executives
Riverside House
High Street, Huntingdon
Cambridgeshire PE18 6SG

Index